An Ocean of Light

An Ocean of Light

Contemplation, Transformation, and Liberation

Martin Laird, O.S.A.

OXFORD
UNIVERSITY PRESS

OXFORD
UNIVERSITY PRESS

Oxford University Press is a department of the University of Oxford. It furthers the University's objective of excellence in research, scholarship, and education by publishing worldwide. Oxford is a registered trade mark of Oxford University Press in the UK and certain other countries.

Published in the United States of America by Oxford University Press 198 Madison Avenue, New York, NY 10016, United States of America.

Library of Congress Cataloging-in-Publication Data
Names: Laird, M. S. (Martin S.), author.
Title: An ocean of light : contemplation, transformation,
and liberation / Martin Laird, O.S.A.
Description: New York, NY, United States of America : Oxford University
Press, 2019. | Includes bibliographical references.
Identifiers: LCCN 2018016578 (print) | LCCN 2018042199 (ebook) |
ISBN 9780199379958 (updf) | ISBN 9780199379965 (epub) |
ISBN 9780199379941 (cloth)
Subjects: LCSH: Contemplation.
Classification: LCC BV5091.C7 (ebook) |
LCC BV5091.C7 L355 2019 (print) | DDC 248.3/4—dc23
LC record available at https://lccn.loc.gov/2018016578

Printed by Sheridan Books, Inc., United States of America

In Memoriam
Dorothy S. Laird
May 16, 1930–January 18, 2018

"May choirs of angels lead you into paradise.
And at your arrival may the martyrs receive and welcome you.
May they bring you home into the Holy City, Jerusalem.
May the holy angels welcome you, and with Lazarus, who lived
in poverty,
may you have everlasting rest."

Contents

Preface

Our lives are rarely as polished as blithesome youth once promised us. Jagged edges abound in even the best-lived lives, and we each have chapters of our lives that are better left unpublished. The arms of the past reach into the present. In the words of the American novelist William Faulkner, "The past is never dead. It's not even past."[1] Although we may not wish to revisit these jagged edges, these unpublished chapters, they serve a purpose: they let in light and love. They are a sign of being made real by love. But didn't we learn all this from the books that formed us as children?

As most grownups come to realize, the themes of really good children's books are aimed directly at the adults who read the book to their own children. Had Margery Williams written but one book, *The Velveteen Rabbit* would have secured her place among the very best writers of works for children. As some of us may remember, when the Boy starts loving any of his stuffed animals, they start to become Real. Because the Boy grew to love the Rabbit very much, the Rabbit, as expected, started the process of becoming Real. This growth made the Rabbit feel confused and out of sorts. The Rabbit turned to the oldest and wisest animal in the nursery, the Skin Horse. "What is REAL?. . . Does it mean having things that buzz inside you and a stick-out handle?" The Skin Horse told the Rabbit that it was not so much like this. "Real isn't how you are made. It's something that happens to you. When a child loves you for a long, long time, not just to play with, but REALLY loves you, then you become Real." The Rabbit wondered if there was pain involved. The Skin Horse told him frankly, "Sometimes." But "When you are Real you don't mind being hurt." The Skin Horse told the Rabbit that the process of becoming Real took time: "It doesn't happen all at once. . . . You become. It takes a long time. That's why it doesn't often happen to people who break easily or have sharp edges, or who have to be carefully kept. Generally, by the time you are Real, most of your hair has been loved off, and your eyes drop out and you get loose in the joints and very shabby." The Rabbit asked the Skin Horse one final question, "I suppose *you* are Real?" The Skin

Horse was not at all bothered by the question, as the Rabbit thought he might be, and replied without hesitation, "The Boy's Uncle made me Real. That was a great many years ago." Finally, the Skin Horse shared with the Rabbit a priceless piece of information, "But once you are Real you can't become unreal again. It lasts for always."[2]

We each uncover different meanings in *The Velveteen Rabbit*, for each of us wears a different skin. For our purposes the following observations have special relevance. Love makes us real. Love creates us and sustains us in the process of realizing who we already are. Love breathes us into being (Gen 2:7). God is divine breath breathing. Humanity the divine breath breathed. How do we separate divine breath breathing from divine breath breathed? They are neither quite the same, nor are they completely different.

Becoming Real is a process. Patience and endurance are required. Hardship and struggle are built into the process of becoming, of realizing who we have always been: living, loving beings whose lives are hidden with Christ in God (Col 3:3). While the Skin Horse tells the Rabbit that becoming Real takes a long while, the Rabbit is already becoming Real, for the Rabbit is already questioning and desiring to become Real.

The Velveteen Rabbit leads us to reflect on our pain and how we relate to it. From this comes the invitation to become aware of other people's pain. We should try as hard as we can to treat other people with the utmost respect simply because each of us is a ray of God's own light; it is sometimes difficult to see that pain is likewise a ray of God's own light, just like every other experience of life whether pleasant or painful. We treat others with reverential respect because we do not know what ordeals they may be facing. They are likely to be uncannily similar to our own.

Jagged edges. Surely the Skin Horse had them, hence his wisdom. And the Rabbit would grow into them. Jagged edges are a sign of our being made real by love. Hence the importance of revisiting the unpublished chapters of our lives. The jagged edges we fear and resist looking at, God has stitched into His very life. The Skin Horse and the Rabbit were stitched together to become themselves. We are stitched into God's very life to become ourselves, selves "hidden with Christ in God" (Col 3:3). And the measure of the best lives lived is quite simply Love, the Love that hovers over the abyss (Gen 1:2).

Mrs. Ramsay also hovers. Among the kindest and sincerest characters in twentieth-century literature is Virginia Woolf's Mrs. Ramsay in *To the Lighthouse*. "Just now . . . she had reached security; she hovered like a hawk suspended; like a flag floated in an element of joy which filled every nerve of her body fully and sweetly, not noisily, solemnly rather, for it arose, she thought . . . from husband and children and friends;

all of which rising in this profound stillness. . . . Nothing need be said; nothing could be said. There it was all around them. It partook, she felt, . . . of eternity."[3] The inner stillness that Mrs. Ramsay perceives is an encounter with eternity. This happens during a meal that she has carefully prepared for those whom she loves in one fashion or another. The eternal God is intimately present yet cannot be pinned down. God is everywhere in such a way that God is at the same time intimately present. *The Velveteen Rabbit* and Mrs. Ramsay in *To the Lighthouse* attest, each in their own way, to the power of love, the love that makes us "Real."

There are some things that love alone can do. Love plumbs depths that our thinking mind cannot, and so must take love's word for it. This distinction does not imply a separation between loving mind and thinking mind. It simply designates areas of expertise. They are ultimately of a piece: love knows what thinking mind loves. Contemplation is the consummation of what it means for us to be made "Real" by love. This consummation includes all our jagged edges—everything about ourselves, published or unpublished, which we resent yet God seeks out as His own abode within us and among us. This gathers love and wound into one: love makes us Real and so do our wounds, indwelled by Love.

The fourteenth-century author of *The Cloud of Unknowing* acknowledges the distinction (not separation) between what our love can do and our thinking mind cannot. The author likens it to having two faculties, a faculty (or capacity) of the thinking, calculating mind and a faculty for loving. God created each of these. However, "God is forever beyond the reach of the first of these, the intellectual faculty; but by means of the second, the loving faculty, [God] can be fully grasped by each individual being."[4] The author clearly values the thinking mind. It is necessary for understanding (grasping with the mind) created beings and "to think clearly about them."[5] Thinking mind functions by means of concepts, images, words, and so on. But God is beyond the grasp of concepts; no word can capture God, no word can have the final word on the Word made flesh, who yet dwells among us (Jn 1:14). "God can well be loved," the author says, "but [God] cannot be thought. By love he can be grasped and held, but by thought neither grasped nor held."[6] God is eternal, the human mind is finite. If God could be comprehended, surrounded by a concept, this would make us greater than God. We invent the illusion that God is a *thing* that we lack and must therefore seek, find, and (attempt to) control.

During the practice of contemplation, we do not cling to thoughts (though they may cling to us) that change like the weather; nor do we cling to the illusory sense of self that is derived from the constant mental movement and mayhem. The practice of contemplation cultivates stillness in our thinking mind, so that it does not dominate the time for prayer, hurling at us all manner of concepts and inner chatter.

The more we give our lives over to the practice of contemplation, the more our thinking mind is trellised by silence, the more easily thinking mind remains still and focused on what it is good at, such as thinking, inventing, writing, creating new ways to hold and heal.

It may sound as if the author of *The Cloud* is getting a bit technical. In truth he is only teasing out some of the subtleties of what Jesus tells us is the greatest and first commandment, "You shall love the Lord, your God, with all your heart, with all your soul, and with all your mind" (Mt 23:37).

God is beyond all telling, yet every tongue tells of God. God's love is not contained by any thought, yet every thought is a dewdrop of Presence. God is embedded in the human heart. Love is our homing instinct to seek God, who is the ground of both our beseeching and our finding. Adam Zagajewski expresses this beautifully in his poem, "Transformation,"

> I've taken long walks
> craving one thing only:
> lightening,
> transformation,
> you.[7]

St. Augustine, the great teacher of love that knows and knowledge that loves, reflects on his own experience of looking for God as an external object, a thing—just huge— that could be located and fixed in space and time. In his

Confessions, he relates how this all changed when he at last forgot himself.

> But when unknown to me you caressed my head,
> and when you closed my eyes lest they see things
> that would seduce me,
> I began for a little while to forget about myself,
> and my madness was lulled to sleep.
> When I awoke in you, I saw you very differently,
> infinite in a very different sense.
> But what I saw was not seen with the eye of the body.[8]

For decades Augustine searched for God where God cannot be found—outside himself in conquest, career, and ambition. Only when God casts him into sleep (Gen 2:21) does something immensely creative happen. Augustine awakes *in* God and beholds what only the inner eye can behold: the traces of God as luminous vastness. As we journey toward the God who causes us to seek, may we discover our own grounding silence and awake in God who has found us from all eternity.

Acknowledgments

Quilting together the pieces of fabric that form this book first began in spring 2015 when I was a recipient of the Yip Fellowship at Magdalene College, Cambridge University. My heartfelt gratitude to the Master and Fellows of Magdalene College for welcoming me into one of the most congenial communities I have ever experienced. Work continued in autumn 2015 when I was a Visiting Fellow at Katholieke Universiteit Leuven. My thanks especially to my academic host, Robertus Faesen, S.J. My writing then ground to a halt for a while as other projects and responsibilities intervened.

Heartfelt thanks to the hundreds of people throughout the United Kingdom, the Republic of Ireland, and the United States who, over the years, have attended many public lectures and retreats. They provided immense help with the quilting. I thank in particular those places whose invitations to return time and again have been generous: Mercy Center, Burlingame, California; the Episcopal House of Prayer, Collegeville, Minnesota; Mepkin Abbey, Moncks Corner, South Carolina; Holy Spirit Monastery, Conyers, Georgia; The Alcyon Center, Mt. Desert Island, Maine; Orlagh Retreat Centre, Rathfarnham, Dublin; The Meditatio Centre, St. Mark's Square, London.

Over the years I have led retreats for most of the Carmelite Monasteries of Nuns in the British Federation, some of these for many years running. I feel humbly grateful to Carmel for being considered "their loving brother." Friendships both old and new—some for quite a few years—have often helped keep me stand upright: Lady Kathleen Buxton; Suzanne Buckley; The Honorable Michael F. X. Coll; Tom and Monica Cornell of The Catholic Worker (who remain the kitchen table of my life and guardians of my basement solitude); Rev. Hampton Deck; Erik Erikson; Fr. Guerric Heckel, monk of Mepkin Abbey; Joan Jordan Grant and Kathryn E. Booth, The Alcyon Center, Seal Cove, Maine; Bro. Elias Marechal, monk of Holy Spirit Monastery; Sr. Mary of St. Joseph,

O.C.D; Betty Maney; Margaret R. Miles; Timothy Shriver; Sr. Susan Toolan, R.S.M. Longstanding gratitude is a precious vintage, and I continue to drink from the cup poured out *"pour la multitude"* by Sr. Carolyn Osiek, R.S.C.J., as well by Werner Valentin, who was an anchor in stormy waters over many years; and to numerous others whom I won't remember until after this book has gone to press.

Gratitude of a rare sort to Dr. Pauline Matarasso. In 1997, while engaged in a period of study at St Benet's Hall, Oxford University, I was "properly introduced" to Pauline Matarasso. Her close friend, Sr. Prue Wilson, R.S.C.J., said to me, "Pauline is one in a million." Sr. Prue did not simply mean Pauline's impressive scholarly prowess. She meant especially the generous integrity of Pauline's person and its rootedness in liturgy and love of neighbor. I still learn much from Pauline of what these things look like concretely as they continue to shine on me as the sun of friendship. Like countless others I dread the day when her sun sets beyond the horizon of our sight (Pauline will rebuke me for writing this paragraph).

Joan Rieck, whom I have known since 1992 (give or take a year), is in a class unto herself. Without even trying she teaches like no one else she teaches that the Silence we seek already shines out our own eyes. You always feel grateful and encouraged even when she rebukes you.

Villanova University has been my academic home for nearly twenty years. I wish to express my gratitude to the erstwhile Dean of the College of Liberal Arts and Science, Rev. Kail Ellis, O.S.A., as well as to the current Dean, Dr. Adele Lindenmeyr, for their patient generosity in giving me the time to bring this book, among other projects, to completion. Likewise, my thanks to my colleagues in the Department of Theology and Religious Studies. It would be a great challenge to find more friendly and collegial colleagues. For the gift of steadfast friendship, I wish to thank especially Dr. Christopher Daly, Dr. Kevin Hughes, and Dr. Thomas Smith.

Finally, my gratitude to the friars and nuns of the Order of St. Augustine, especially The Very Reverend Bernard C. Scianna, O.S.A., erstwhile Prior Provincial of the Chicago Province. Throughout his terms of office, he has been a listening ear, quick to respond, and a port in a storm. St. Monica's Priory, Hoxton Square, London, has offered me, for over twenty years, hospitality of a rare sort, especially Fr. Paul Graham, O.S.A., and Fr. Mark Minihane, O.S.A. The early morning and early evening silent prayer kept my hidden life in the Priory healing and whole. Between the Priory and the British Library (two stops up on the Northern Line), the final version of virtually every book or article I have published has been completed and printed off in the Priory. I also wish to thank Mother Mary Grace, O.S.A., Fr. Richard Jacobs, O.S.A., Fr. Gerald Nicholas, O.S.A., Fr. Benignus O'Rourke, O.S.A., Fr. James Thomson, O.S.A., as well as departed confrères, who from beyond the grave continue to bestow grace, prudence, and perspective: Fr. John J. FitzGerald, O.S.A.; Fr. Raymond R. Ryan, O.S.A.; Rev. Theodore E. Tack, O.S.A.

Finally, I must thank my brothers and sisters, Rob, Cece, Lindsay, and Scott, as we reconfigure our respective lives together after mom's death, who previously did all the configuring that could possibly be done.

I cannot imagine a more generous, supportive, talented, and patient editor than Cynthia Read at Oxford University Press. Her steadying and humane support were especially needed during challenging times. My thanks also to Drew Anderla and Carl Vennerstrom for their technical assistance and support. Without Elizabeth Wales these three volumes on contemplation would never have found a home at Oxford University Press. Her encouragement throughout has been deeply sustaining.

All these debts of gratitude will never be paid back; for they are such a pleasure to bear.

Biblical citations, if not from memory, are from various English translations: the *New Jerusalem Bible*; the *New*

American Bible; the *New Revised Standard Version*; the *Liturgy of the Hours*.

Among the various ways to express our concerns to heal sexist language, I continue to use the transcendent upper-case to refer to God (no doubt this practice has the least cachet). Moreover, I continue to make judicious use of the passive voice. The passive voice can be enormously helpful, despite the "convention" many of us were taught infallibly to use the passive voice only as a last resort. To me this convention never seemed as infallible as it was presented in school. After all, it exists in every tense, mood, and voice. The press uses the passive voice routinely to avoid being held accountable for anything they say: "It is said that . . ." "It is thought that . . ." If the press can use the passive voice to dodge responsibility in reporting news that is not yet known to be true or false (or real), we can use it successfully, if sparingly and always with an ear to rhythm and euphony, to heal sexist language. One could go on.

Grateful thanks to Farrar, Straus, and Giroux for permission to quote from Adam Zagajewski, *Without End: New and Selected Poems*, translated by Clare Cavanaugh, Renata Gorczynski, Benjamin Ivry, and C. K. Williams; University of Notre Dame Press for permission to quote from Kevin Hart, *Morning Knowledge*; Many Rivers Press for permission to quote from David Whyte, *River Flow: New and Selected*

Poems; Alfred A. Knopf for permission to quote from Franz Wright, *Walking to Martha's Vineyard*; *God's Silence*; *Wheeling Motel*; Bloodaxe Books, Ltd., for permission to quote from R. S. Thomas, *Collected Later Poems 1988–2000*; The Orion Publishing Group for permission to quote from R. S. Thomas, *Collected Poems 1945–1990* (J. M. Dent, an imprint of The Orion Publishing Group).

An Ocean of Light

PART I

ONE

Thoughts with a Thousand Arms

Contemplation and the Human Condition

Don't try to keep silence, just listen.
— Madeleine Delbrêl, *Alcide*

Everything is constantly changing; nothing remains static.
— Thaddeus of Vitovnica

There is a coherence in things; a stability.
— Virginia Woolf, *To the Lighthouse*

In a commencement address delivered to the 2005 graduating class at Kenyon College, David Foster Wallace begins, as any novelist would, with a story that speaks to the human condition. "There are these two young fish swimming along, and they happen to meet an older fish swimming the other way, who nods at them and says, 'Morning, boys, how's the water?' And the two young fish swim on for a bit, and then eventually one of them looks at the other and goes, 'What the hell is water?'"[1] A simple enough story. An older and presumably wiser fish is completely aware of his surroundings, while the two younger fish are completely unaware of their surroundings.

Self-absorbed mental numbness is far easier to slip into than we might like to think. As Wallace sees it, self-centeredness is our default setting and is "hard-wired into our boards at birth."[2] He continues, "There is no experience you've had that you were not the absolute center of."[3] At the same time, he wants to reassure us that he is not going to be lecturing about compassion or other-directedness or the so-called virtues. "This is not a matter of virtue—it's a matter of my choosing to do the work of somehow altering or getting free of my natural, hard-wired default-setting, which is to be deeply and literally self-centered, and to see and interpret everything through this lens of self."[4]

Education should help us move beyond simply listening to ourselves talk to ourselves, listening to a great monologue going on in our head. " 'Learning how to think' really means learning how to exercise some control over *how* and *what* you think."[5] This is the real value of a liberal arts education. The essence of learning how to think is "being conscious and aware enough to choose what you pay attention to. . . . How to keep from going through your comfortable, prosperous, respectable adult life dead, unconscious, a slave to your head and to your natural default-setting of being uniquely, completely imperially alone, day in and day out."[6]

Cultivating the skill of becoming aware of our thoughts allows for the possibility of choosing what we give our attention to. This awareness plays itself out in practical ways. Wallace uses the often frustrating experience of buying groceries as an example. The mayhem of the crowds, the frustration of waiting in line until it is finally our turn to pay, dealing with the chaos of the parking lot can easily trigger a deluge of self-centered inner chatter. Wallace says, "Thinking this way is my natural default-setting. It's the automatic, unconscious way that I experience the boring, frustrating, crowded parts of adult life when I'm operating on the automatic, unconscious belief that I am the center of the world and that my immediate needs and feelings are what should determine the world's priorities."[7] By learning to choose what we give our attention to we open ourselves up to the possibilities of experiencing a situation with less anxiety and with more compassion. "But if you've really learned how to think, how to pay attention, then you will know you have other options."[8] This will liberate us by giving us more mental space so that we can ask ourselves, "How might other people (life itself) be other than our self-centered default setting thinks it is?" In Wallace's case he is freed up enough to direct his attention within and ask himself, for example, if the woman who is annoying him so much by screaming at her child might in fact "have been up three nights straight holding the hand of her husband who's dying of bone cancer."[9] In this case the screaming would be more understandable. We need to cultivate the habit of being aware of our thoughts as they arise and choosing which ones really merit our attention. When we can unseat or reset the default setting of deeply ingrained self-centeredness we widen our capacity to interrogate our own thinking.

In the end Wallace offers no adequate medicament for the human predicament. However, he points us in the right direction, the grace of worship. "There is no such thing as not worshipping. Everybody worships. The only choice we get is *what* to worship. And an outstanding reason for choosing some sort of God or spiritual-type thing to worship—be it J. C. or Allah, be it Allah or the Wiccan mother-goddess or . . . some infrangible set of ethical principles—is that pretty much anything else will eat you alive."[10] Wallace gets a bit vague here, advocating the choice of "some sort of God or spiritual-type thing" in order to avoid the dangerous consequences of not doing so—a sort of Pascal's wager with most of the air let out.

The predicament Wallace depicts is one that is well known throughout the Christian tradition. In her private journal, Flannery O'Connor, the twentieth century's great master of the American short story, writes, "I do not know You God because I am in the way."[11] David Foster Wallace likewise knows he is in the way. But there is a crucial difference between O'Connor and Wallace on this point. O'Connor is addressing God. Her realization that she gets "in the way" is the fruit of being *in a living and loving relationship* with God. Wallace, by contrast, seems to think that we ourselves, by simply being aware, can change these deeply ingrained, habituated patterns of self-centeredness. Our role is necessary, yes, but it is insufficient on its own. Later in this book we shall have occasion to see the unbidden emergence of grace within the life of the young Dutch Jewish writer Etty Hillesum.

For Wallace we are ultimately left alone to manage our default setting, "I am the center of the universe." However, the self-centered person who attempts to reset his or her own default setting *knows nothing other than the default setting*. The default setting is thus simply replaced by another version of the same default setting. The result is that we continue to reject what we don't want and cling to what we do want. This pattern of rejecting and clinging actually undergirds the default setting. The deeper question we need to ask is, "What is the nature of these thoughts that we either cast aside or hold on to?" This question is not answered by our thinking mind, but by means of our inner silence, which has been cultivated over several years of practicing inner silence (the practice of contemplation). Inner silence leads to a different sort of realization: thoughts in themselves (be they self-centered or other-oriented) are completely see-through. They are not real in the way we once took them to be. The inner chatter in our heads, with which Wallace is well familiar, gives our thoughts their narrative grip. Our own inner silence, cultivated in a relationship that is by nature prayer, reveals the apparent solidity of our thoughts to be illusory.

Despite Wallace's assertions, we simply cannot pull this off by ourselves. What we alone can do we cannot do alone. Hence, something that Christianity calls grace (God as constantly giving, constantly pouring Himself out) is an *utterly reliable necessity.* As we shall see in the writings of Howard Thurman, the famous American preacher, theologian, confidante, and mentor to Dr. Martin Luther King, Jr., the grace of religious experience is a question of being free to enjoy God "coming to Himself in me. . . . In that glorious and transcendent moment, it may easily seem to me that all there is, is God."[12] Thurman is not the center of his own experience. The center is God. Without this graced dimension of self-forgetful receptivity, what Wallace genuinely wishes for each of us will not hold. There will be no transformation or liberation because Wallace's default setting will return to the only things it knows. Someone who would have been in agreement with much of Wallace's critique, but who took things to a far deeper level, is the twentieth-century Trappist monk Thomas Merton, who despite his untimely death in 1968 remains a spiritual prophet for the early decades of the twenty-first century, just as he was for the second half of the twentieth.

Composed over fifty years ago, "Contemplation in a World of Action" remains one of Merton's most important essays. Wallace acknowledges our need to have sufficient skills of interiority in order to become aware of our own self-centered patterns of thinking and behaving. He likewise realizes that we can actually choose what we give our attention to. In choosing to give our attention to something other than the monologues going on in our heads, we meet the possibility of becoming less self-centered and more compassionate people. Merton would have no problem with Wallace on this point, but Merton would say that we have to go yet deeper—journey much deeper into our own uncharted lands. Wallace teaches us to clear away some of the underbrush but he does not seem to be aware of what is required for us to stride forth into the uncharted, inner landscape of the spirit. As Merton puts it, "Without a more profound human understanding derived from exploration of the inner ground of human existence, love will tend to be superficial and deceptive."[13] Wallace sees the superficial and delusional aspects of our lives and loves, but he himself has not broken through into the "inner ground" of life. Merton reminds us that the skills of "meditation and contemplation have [traditionally] been associated with this deepening of one's personal life and this expansion of the capacity to understand and serve others."[14] For Merton a life of contemplation (monastery walls or not) will necessarily involve our encounter with the *inner ground of human existence.*

What Wallace suggests is easily recognized as a type of ancient contemplative discipline called "vigilance" or "watchfulness." The cultivation of inner vigilance requires our becoming far more intimately aware of the thoughts we are having than Wallace is aware of. The fourth-century desert monk Evagrius Ponticus was an immensely skilled teacher of inner vigilance.[15] In fact, as we shall see, Evagrius requires us to become far more adept than Wallace suggests. Awareness of our thought-feelings as they rise and fall is training for something else: loving union with God through contemplation. For Evagrius, inner vigilance is necessary but insufficient for contemplation. For after learning how to be aware of our thoughts, what sets them off? Do they team up or do that act solo? Do some pose us greater difficulty than others? Under what conditions are we more vulnerable to certain afflictive thoughts, and when are we less vulnerable to their attacks?—*we must then learn to let these thoughts go* in order to enter the vast, open countryside whose name is prayer. As Evagrius puts it in his characteristically cryptic manner, "prayer is the letting go of thoughts."[16]

Merton suggests that contemplation, the "inner awareness of God's direct presence becomes not so much a matter of cause and effect as a celebration of love. In the light of this celebration, what matters most is love itself, thankfulness, assent to the unbounded and overflowing goodness of love which comes from God and reveals [God] to the world."[17] The opening up of awareness to "God's direct presence," and our assent to the "overflowing goodness of love," are not separate discoveries or separate events in time; first one then the other. They occur simultaneously. Without this realization of the direct presence, Merton assures us, we "will have nothing to give others. [We] will communicate to them nothing but the contagion of [our] own obsessions, aggressiveness, ego-centered ambitions and delusions about ends and means."[18] Human interiority and its full-flowering as contemplation have a vitally important role "in opening up new ways and new horizons."[19]

On October 11, 2012, the 104th Archbishop of Canterbury, Dr. Rowan Williams, addressed the Synod of Bishops in Rome.[20] In an address both inspired and inspiring, Williams reminds the bishops of the absolute centrality of contemplation to human aliveness in Christ. "The humanity we are growing into in the Spirit, the humanity that we seek to share with the world as the first fruit of Christ's redeeming work, is a *contemplative humanity*."[21] Williams goes on to say something that must have been startling for some of the bishops: "Contemplation is very far from being just one kind of thing Christians do: it is the key to prayer, liturgy, art and ethics, the key to the essence of a renewed humanity that is capable of seeing the world and other subjects in the world with freedom—freedom from self-oriented, acquisitive habits and the distorted understanding that comes from them."[22] He continues, "To put it boldly, contemplation is the only ultimate answer to the unreal and insane world that our financial systems and our advertising culture and our chaotic and unexamined emotions encourage us to inhabit. To learn contemplative practice is to learn what we need so as to live truthfully and honestly and lovingly."[23] In this challenging statement which Williams makes to the Roman Catholic bishops gathered in synod, we can hear distant echoes of Merton. Without a humanity shaped by contemplation, "[We] will have nothing to give others. [We] will communicate to them nothing but the contagion of [our] own obsessions, aggressiveness, ego-centered ambitions and delusions about ends and means."[24] The marketing and advertising cultures pervade our culture and invade our spiritual lives. The practice of contemplation is not beyond the reach of their greed. Spiritual greed and the forces of the market economy turn spirituality in general into an industry, a product that sits on a shelf and sells well. Even more sadly, this culture reinforces an already deeply ingrained, habituated conviction that we are separate from God as from an object. We therefore think we need a spiritual strategy, such as the practice of contemplation, to acquire something that has never been entirely lost to begin with; once acquired (or so we think), we possess it. Once possessed, we attempt to control what we think a spiritual life should look like. Spirituality is co-opted into a highly attractive, egoic enterprise. Rowan Williams states the matter as boldly as it can be, "It [contemplation] is a deeply revolutionary matter."[25]

Contemplation is crucial to that human thriving and wholeness found in the transcendent intimacy we call God. The gift of contemplation transforms and liberates our heart in a host of ways: (1) contemplation dispels the illusion that we are separate from God; (2) it gives birth to the simple realization that God is the all-loving, groundless ground of being; (3) insofar as we are, we are in God; (4) contemplation liberates us from the illusions that dominate, confuse, and stunt human thriving; (5) it frees us from the illusion that God is an object we lack and therefore need to seek; (6) contemplation liberates us from the seeds of violence in our own heart, especially from our individual and social compulsions to find someone to blame for the ills that befall us—such compulsions do nothing but keep us bent over on ourselves, blind to what constitutes a human.

The practice of contemplation is good not only for us but also for the entire world. Many testimonies throughout the contemplative tradition bear witness to this. Not least among these is that of the author of *The Cloud of Unknowing*: "This is the work [the practice of contemplation] of the soul that pleases God most. All the saints and angels rejoice in this work and hasten to help it with all their might. All the devils are driven crazy when you do this and try to frustrate it in all the ways they can. All people living on earth are marvelously helped by this work, in ways you do not know. Yes, even the souls in purgatory are relieved of their pain by the power of this work."[26]

Some contemplatives have understood their own role in the spiritual order of things as extending even beyond this life. St. Elizabeth of the Trinity writes, "I think that in Heaven my mission will be to draw souls by helping them go out of themselves to cling to God by a wholly simple and loving movement, and to keep them in this great silence within that will allow God to communicate Himself and transform them into Himself."[27]

In our own time, the twentieth-century Serbian monk Thaddeus of Vitnovnica writes, "If our thoughts are kind, peaceful, and quiet, turned only toward good, then we also influence ourselves and radiate peace all around us—in our family, the whole country, everywhere. This is true not only here on earth, but in the cosmos as well. When we labor in the fields of the Lord, we create harmony. Divine harmony, peace, and quiet spread everywhere."[28] This Serbian speaks with great conviction that silence lies within each of us. But he is likewise aware of the destructive nature of our clinging to thoughts that have little to do with love, peace, and justice within people and among peoples. "However, when we breed negative thoughts, that is a great evil. When there is evil in us, we radiate it among our family members, and wherever we go. . . . Destructive thoughts destroy the stillness within, and then we have no peace."[29] The apostolic dimension of contemplation never diminishes and places us at the heart of the spiritual balance of the universe.

There remain a startling number of people who, for one reason or another, think that the contemplative life is, at worse, an irrelevancy that somehow implies being cut off from and unconcerned with the world and its concerns and, at best, something to which very few among us are called. The saints and sages of the Christian contemplative tradition (non-Christian contemplative traditions as well) have long known that such a scenario is not in the realm of possibility. As the poet Franz Wright has expressed it, "The road to Emmaus is this world."[30] Contemplation is a word that describes the most subtly significant thing that can happen to a person before death and through death. It is the consummation in God of both life and death. St Elizabeth of the Trinity states this, with both concision and stunning orthodoxy, "He is your soul and your soul is He."[31]

In the spirit of David Foster Wallace, Flannery O'Connor, Howard Thurman, Evagrius, Thomas Merton, Rowan Williams, St. Elizabeth of the Trinity, and a host of others whom the reader will meet either for the first time or rejoice in seeing old friends again, we offer the present volume. From the Christian point of view, contemplation reveals our immersion in the mystery of God in Christ, where St. Paul says our lives are hidden (Col 3:3) and where God is revealed as the Being of our being; the Love of our loving; the Life of our living. The mystery of God in Christ seeks to bring Himself to others through us, as food for the hungry, clothing for the naked, justice for the imprisoned, and compassion for the stranger, the widow, and the orphan. Contemplation, and the lifestyle leading to it and flowing from it, asks but a single question, "What does kindness look like at any given moment?"

This book serves as a companion volume to the two preceding it, *Into the Silent Land* and *A Sunlit Absence* (knowledge of the previous books is not a prerequisite for reading this book). The first volume addresses a certain need in the literature on contemplation. There are a number of good books on contemplation. However, at the time there were not many books written with intermediates in mind, that is, those who already had a very well-established practice going. While there is enough in *Into the Silent Land* to bring along beginners (aren't we all?), that book focuses very much on those who already have a well-established practice and could meet the challenges we all face with the support of this already maturing practice. *A Sunlit Absence* was written with the same readership in mind, but with a focus on some of the more challenging (often defeating) themes that we typically meet a bit later in a maturing practice. In fact these challenges

can appear whenever loving Providence deems it appropriate: boredom for example. Paralyzing boredom in (and
with) the practice of contemplation is a given in any maturing
practice and can begin settling in quite early. When boredom
begins its excavating work of deepening our practice, we can
sometimes think we have lost our prayer lives, or even our
entire faith. This is often what will get people springing off
their prayer benches in search of a type of prayer that has a
bit more juice. To the extent that this newly discovered way
of prayer is genuine, we will normally be led back to desert
dryness. We don't normally get rid of dryness so much as we
stop demanding that it goes away. Spiritual aridity is the natural terrain of stillness.

The nature of awareness features strongly in *A Sunlit
Absence* and is presented with a view to weaning our attention away from what we are aware *of* to awareness itself—the
very aware-ing. The mind automatically resists this, and so
we hear people say such things as, "I'm aware of my awareness." Awareness itself cannot be turned into an object except
by way of deceptive trickery. *A Sunlit Absence* also discusses
the fact that silence does not simply mean the absence of
sound waves.

For the quiet mind even irritating noise throngs with silence.
Obviously we have a clear preference of one over the other.
The book also looks at some of the "intellectual purifications."
These liberations target the higher spiritual faculties, especially

pride or the clinging mind. Searing and painful and lasting as long as it needs to and returning as required, it is all accomplished by very loving Light.

The present volume, *An Ocean of Light*, develops certain themes from the previous volumes and introduces new ones but explores them from a different angle and in greater detail. Part I develops yet further and more emphatically the illusion of being separate from God. We do this by simply allowing the great cloud of witness of the contemplative tradition to have a voice. While differing one from the other—different centuries, life contexts, cultures, gender, and language, together they sing in harmony, polyphony, and descant the song of union. If God were not already the ground of our being, the divine breath breathing us into being, we would not exist.

God does not know how to be absent. That is to say, it would go against God's nature for God to come and go. But we can be ignorant of this intimate presence and build a lifestyle that maintains this ignorance. St. Augustine provides a hint as to why we experience as absent what is actually intimately present. As we have often heard this monk-bishop put it, "You are closer to me than I am to myself."[32] God is too close to us for our eyes to notice. The problem is not that God is absent but that God is so intimately present. If we are frightened to look within for fear of what we might find there, we will never be at home within ourselves, never at ease in our own skin. If we are not at home within ourselves, we will never realize that we live in the house of the Father in whom there are many dwelling places (Jn 14:2).

What prevents us from realizing what is so simply and intimately present? There are theological attempts to answer this that have been passed on down through the centuries. But from a more practical view, that of the practice of contemplation, we can say that our vision is somehow cluttered. As a result we may find ourselves judging others out of our own ignorance of what life is like for them, the tremendous struggles they might be going through. Jesus' response to this situation is among his most famous, "Stop judging, that you may not be judged. For as you judge, so will you be judged, and the measure with which you measure will be measured out to you. Why do you notice the splinter in your brother's or sister's eye but do not perceive the wooden beam in your own eye?" (Mt 7:1–4). The problem is that our vision is heavily lumbered, our minds deeply cluttered. Part II uses this metaphor of the cluttering and decluttering of our minds as a way of considering how the practice of contemplation works. The metaphor allows us to look at the contemplative process of liberation from a point of view other than that of acquiring something we think we do not have and therefore must come up with a strategy to acquire, possess, and control.

Think of a bright and spacious room whose polished wooden floor is covered with mounds of clutter of whatever sort. The practice of contemplation gradually declutters our minds, gradually revealing the brightly polished floor—the radiant core of all—that we did not realize was already there. This book avoids the use of *the* mind to avoid giving the impression that mind is a state or something static. We sometimes speak of mind as though it were a state. Someone might say to us, "Come back when I'm in a better state of mind." In fact, however, mind (or mindstream) has a thousand arms that are in constant motion. Mind is forever changing; it's never fixed or permanent. Here we will highlight three manifestations of mind: reactive, receptive, and luminous. We consider the same questions with respect to each: What is practice like? What is ego like? What contemplative skills are developing? What are some special challenges?

Our guiding metaphor of clutter and the process of decluttering (release, letting be, letting go, non-clinging) bring to the fore certain topics crucial to the practice of contemplation that are sometimes passed by with little notice by the many good books on contemplation that emphasize growth, development, progress, acquiring something we think we lack. Some of these are (1) the futility of our concern with our own progress; (2) using the allure of the contemplative path as a way of keeping God at bay; (3) overemphasis on being mindful *of* or aware *of* objects in our awareness, which has a vital but *transitional* role—if mindfulness stops here we will hinder the blossoming of our practice as the naked simplicity of direct pointing to the luminous vastness;

(4) luminous vastness cannot be an object of awareness, for it is the radiant ground of all that is; (5) focusing on our own progress, growth, and development leads very easily to our remaining objects of our own fascination—ourselves as our own contemplative projects.

Part III addresses the topic of depression, especially depression that does not go away as the scientific research on meditation says it should. Depression can leave many of us completely flattened or worse: thrashing in the quicksand of stigma, where we worsen our condition by our attempts to be free of it. This final chapter seeks to show that the practice of contemplation reveals the possibility of profound service to all who suffer from depression. Our own dereliction and defeat can become a bridge for all those who have no bridge.

The observations and reflections in this book are but paper boats on the river. Perhaps one or two will make landfall with you.

TWO

Silence Shining Like the Sun

The Song of Union

The people who lived in darkness have seen a great light.
—Isaiah 9:2; Matthew 4:16

Because I have a voice!
—*The King's Speech*

Christ is the I of our I.
—St. Irenaeus

INTRODUCTION: LIGHT SITTING IN LIGHT

"How can you see with all that light?" So exclaims the twentieth-century American author Dorothy Parker (1893–1967). Famed for her caustic wit and cocktailed conversations with other élite writers of her day, Parker was blind drunk the night before and is recovering from quite a hangover. In her present state she simply cannot bear the light of day. Parker's predicament differs notably from the enlightening experience of the liberated prisoner in Plato's famous "Allegory of the Cave."[1] When at long last he emerges, purged and freed of shadowed ignorance, the only reality he has ever known, he must first shield his eyes from the sun until he gradually grows accustomed to the sunlit splendor of the Good.

The light that Dorothy Parker cannot bear likewise differs from the light that Jesus manifests: "the radiant light of God's glory" (Heb 1:3). Or the luminous splendor that Jesus manifests when "after six days he took Peter and James and John his brother, and led them up by themselves up the high mountain. And there he was transfigured before them. And his face shone like the sun. And his garments became white as light" (Mt 17:1–9).

There is the light that brings St. Paul (then still called Saul) to a sudden halt on his way to Damascus when "suddenly a heavenly light flashed about him, and he fell to the ground" (Acts 9:3–4). St. Paul is blind for three days as a result of his encounter with the Divine Light of the Risen One. Paul is not blind drunk, but blinded by Light. Paul is gradually integrated into this Divine Light, which becomes the driving force of his entire life and mission. Moreover, this Divine Light becomes something so intimately bound up with Paul's identity that when Paul turns his gaze within he does not see anyone there named Paul. Hence, his jubilant realization, "I have been crucified with Christ. It is no longer I who live but

Christ living in me" (Gal 2:20). St. Paul looks within and sees not himself but Christ.

GREAT PEALS OF LIGHT:
A CHOIR OF UNION

This Mystery, luminous and intimate, has kissed the lives of the great saints and sages of the contemplative tradition; they realize that this creating and sustaining Mystery is likewise the Light-soaked ground that is foundational to being human, foundational to light, life, and love. This luminous Mystery also kisses the lives of each of us, else we would not exist.

Union with God is not something we can or need to acquire. By way of the contemplative skills of engaged receptivity and release, we realize this Union ever more deeply and clearly throughout the course of the days given us. God is too simple to be absent. It is we who, with complicated and cluttered minds, remain unaware that this foundational Light is flowering perpetually in the fertile and unfathomable *right now*. As St. Augustine wrote in his *Confessions*: You are "more intimate to me than my inmost self."[2] Paraphrasing this very line, Meister Eckhart preaches: "The soul takes her being immediately from God: therefore God is nearer to the soul than she is to herself, and therefore God is in the ground of the soul with all His Godhead."[3] St. Augustine likewise knows this grounding light: "This light itself is one, and all those who see it and love it are one."[4]

This chapter allows us to listen. We listen to a Song of Union sung down the ages by the choir of those who have gone deeply into the pathless Path of contemplative realization. Each of us has a voice in this choir, but due to the din of inner noise streaming in our heads, we live largely deaf to our own voices singing this Song of Union that sings of ourselves ever hidden in God. This choir likewise attests to the intimacy of this foundational union, sung throughout the centuries in different times and places. Because this that we call a self is ever hidden, we can never see it or chart it as an object of our awareness, for it is the sustaining ground of awareness, *the aware-ing itself* shining out of our own eyes. At the same time, it grounds the ever-expanding joy at the sight of the beautiful uniqueness of the characters of each one of us. This delight that dilates the heart reveals the simple suchness of all creation. In the arithmetic of divine union, one plus one equals "not even one." Without this grounding union we could never perceive the particular dynamism in the created identity of all evolving creation.

The fourth-century bishop and theologian St. Gregory of Nyssa affirms that "God dwells in you, penetrates you yet is not confined in you."[5] Here he echoes the Psalmist: "Lord, you search me and you know me. . . . For you formed me in my inmost being and knitted me together in my mother's womb . . . as I was being fashioned in secret" (Ps 139). The searching, sifting presence of God comes as God's initiative. It is not something we need to seek, for it is already given us as Gift from all eternity. We become ever more present to this Presence only by way of release and receptivity. Not through the calculating grasp of acquisition. We don't drive around town in search of our own nostrils. Even though we can't see them somehow we trust, drive home, and put the car back in the garage.

The fourth-century theologian and bishop St. Ambrose of Milan sings of this divine intimacy in the language of Divine rest. In his *Commentary on the Days of Creation*, Ambrose explains why God waited until the final day of creation to create the human. "Surely it is time now for us to make our contribution of silence, for now God rests from his work in making the world. God has found repose in the deep recesses of humanity, in humanity's mind and purpose. . . . God finds comfort in these traits, as his own testimony declares, 'in whom shall I find repose but in the human who is humble and peaceful.' "[6] From the perspective of theology, creation is not concerned with something that happened a long time ago; rather it betokens a sustaining relationship in the present moment, the full-flowering of human identity that remains something ever hidden in the Mystery of Christ in God (Col 3:3). For

St. Ambrose, the ineffable truth of human identity is that we are God's Sabbath. There is but one Sabbath and that is God's.

An often overlooked spiritual master and theologian of the early middle ages, John Scottus Eriugena, or simply Eriugena (810–877), is the outstanding spiritual teacher of the ninth century. In his *Homily on the Prologue to the Gospel of St. John*, Eriugena writes of John, "He would not have ascended to God if he had not first become God."[7] This is also true of each of us, but not in such a way that if we looked into a mirror we would see anything but a stubble of beard or eyebrows in need of color and perhaps a chemical peel thrown in. Eriugena is simply speaking of the translucent realization of the true nature of our innermost depths. Divinization or *theosis* is an ancient theological term for this (see 2 Peter 1; 4). Perhaps the most famous statement of this is provided by St. Athanasius the Great, "God became human so that humans may become God."[8] What God is by nature we become by grace.

Again St. Augustine provides useful insight when he states simply, "You cannot love what you do not know."[9] If we desire something we must somehow have known it. No one desires plaid-flavored ice cream because it does not exist. Humans don't typically long for things that don't exist. Do you desire to have the same haircut as the Martian you saw at the mall last month?

If we experience a longing for God, Truth, Beauty, Happiness, the Peace and Silence that have no opposite, then we have in some hidden way known God, and for this hidden knowledge to have taken place, God must first have known us in some hidden way. Our very longing for God is a *response* to having already been touched and embraced by God. Desire is but our homing instinct for God, even when there is static, confusion, and missing of the mark yet again. "You have made us for yourself, O Lord," Augustine says, "and our heart is restless until it rests in you."[10] Augustine hears the distant echoes of the Psalmist, "In God alone is my soul at rest" (Ps 61:1).

The fourteenth century boasts of numerous spiritual masters. Among those who loom especially large are Meister Eckhart and Jan van Ruusbroec. Pope St. John Paul II cites Meister Eckhart in one of his weekly audiences: "Did not Eckhart teach his disciples: 'All that God asks you most pressingly is to go out of yourself . . . and let God be God in you'?"[11] This Dominican friar preaches: "God's ground is my ground and my ground is God's ground."[12] In an Advent Sermon, Eckhart says: "God constantly introduces a strong light into the soul. . . . In this birth God pours himself into the soul with light so much that it spills over into the faculties and the outer self."[13] Eckhart is saying that sometimes this Light dawns from within the light of awareness so strongly that we have an abiding sense of gazing into a great luminous vastness. We also become aware that what gazes into luminous vastness is itself luminous vastness. Maturing contemplatives would see this as an example of what happened to Paul: "God bathed him in his light as he journeyed."[14] Or when the fourth-century desert monk Evagrius Ponticus says: "The proof of *apatheia* (a bedrock peace which, like silence, has no opposite) is had when the mind begins to see its own light and when it . . . remains in abiding calm as it beholds the affairs of life."[15] "As it beholds the affairs of life" is classic understatement; for *apatheia* grounds our bouts of depression, health crises that come suddenly out of nowhere, the pain of a difficult divorce, the unexpected loss of a stillborn child, as well as our joys and triumphs, even our most successes and petty concerns—the entirety of our lives as they happen to be. We have little problem with perceiving God's light and will in the positive things that come our way; but most of us have a rather more difficult time realizing what the Psalmist knew, "darkness and light are both the same in you" (Ps 139:12). Whether in despair or delight we release into and rest in the fullness of God (though we clearly have our preferences).

Eckhart speaks from what he himself personally knows: "We are [read I am] well aware of this light. Whenever we turn to God there is a light that burns in us, guiding us."[16] We must "know," says Eckhart, "that the very best and noblest attainment in this life is to be silent and let God work and speak within."[17]

The fourteenth-century Flemish spiritual master and theologian, Blessed Jan van Ruusbroec, likewise stands luminous and grand among the theological giants of his age and also, like Meister Eckhart, throughout the centuries that follow. In an often undervalued work, *The Little Book of Clarification*, which in many ways serves as a summary of his thought, Ruusbroec says that for the Enlightened, "In the same way that the air is pervaded with the radiance and warmth of the sun or a piece of iron is penetrated by fire, so that with the fire it does the work of fire, burning and giving light just as fire does . . . yet each retains its own nature—for the fire does not become iron, nor the iron fire, *but the union is without intermediary*, for the iron is within the fire and the fire within the iron, even as the air is in the light of the sun and the light of the sun is in the air—so too is God constantly in the being of the soul."[18] Elsewhere he writes that after sufficient preparation by Grace, "we will flow forth and flow out of ourselves into the incomprehensible abundance of the presence of God's riches and goodness. In it we will also melt and be dissolved, revolve and be eternally whirled around in the maelstrom of God's glory."[19] Ruusbroec emphasizes what all of his forebears realized and what Ruusbroec himself knew: "This grace flows from within not from without, for God is more interior to us than we are to ourselves."[20]

St. Catherine of Genoa (1447–1510) adds another voice to the Song of Union. She is well known for her startling realization of her own identity hidden in God. St. Catherine simply says "My only 'me' is God." She continues, "In my soul I see nothing but God."[21] She is well aware that she can't go around saying to every passerby, "Psst! Do you know who I really am?" But this is how life seems to her. When the illusion of separation from God drops, this is how life looks to someone whose daily life is ever more integrated into the single, open gaze of unitive awareness. Catherine's sense of "normal" is now a unitive awareness as she goes about her daily round of caring for the sick and orphaned of Genoa, for these likewise manifest the formless as form. The term "unitive awareness" means that grounding, luminous awareness that perceives no opposites such as true self versus false self, non-dual versus dual awareness, gay versus straight, "not Jew or Greek, not slave or free, not male and female for [we] are all one in Christ" (Gal 3:28). Yet all the while these apparent opposites each manifest the same ocean of light. Unitive awareness knows only how to be: one, or better, *not even one.* It is not something countable or contained by the conceptual domain of mathematics. Yet, lest the theological thought-police of her day (or ours) applies for an arrest warrant for a collapsed theology of creation, St. Catherine (and each of us) manifests the brimming *realization* of what it means to evolve into the fullness of our createdness, the shimmering suchness of all creation.

The brightest beacon of sixteenth-century Spain is the towering figure of St. Teresa of Avila. The purpose of a beacon is not to produce light for itself but to provide light by which others may see. This is clearly the case with St. Teresa. Her most famous work is *The Interior Castle*. As readers, we expect her to reserve her discussion of divine union until the Seventh and final Dwelling Place, where divine union and service to our neighbor are one and the same. In the Seventh Dwelling Place she does indeed address divine union. Her own unitive awareness affords her the gracious space to wrap words around how life and love appear to her now. "In total Union," she says, "no separation is possible. The soul remains perpetually in that center. . . . [It] is like rain falling into a river or pool; there is nothing but water. It is impossible to divide the sky-water from the land water. When a little stream enters the sea, who could separate its waters back out again? Think of a bright light pouring into a room from two large windows: it enters from different places but becomes one light."[22] For all the gratitude we owe the dualist mind for the beauty and creativity of reasoning, investigating, distinguishing, for scientific inquiry that prods the wondrous subtleties of the world and all manner of contribution to life, art, and culture, this dualist (thinking) mind does not have the final word on what counts as real or normal. With the

blossoming of the eye of the heart, the unitive gaze of awareness itself, not something we are aware of but the *aware-ing
itself*, life and love present themselves in a profoundly simple
manner. It is never a case of blurring the intellectual distinction of Creator and creation (who would want to?), but rather
one of unfathomable insight into their inseparable bond (even
these words fail). But the blossoms of awareness, these petals
of mind, allow Teresa to describe what life looks like from
the unitive gaze of mind's full-flowering from *within* awareness. Nevertheless, Teresa insists that what can be said of the
Seventh Dwelling Place can be said of the First. She says that
this divine light is present from the very foundation of our
search. In the First Dwelling Place, she insists, "The soul is
innately capable of sharing this divine light as a crystal is in
reflecting the radiance of the sun. . . . The fountainhead that
shines like the sun from the center of the soul *never loses its
beauty*."[23] Further on in the First Dwelling, Teresa continues,
"It is as if a person were to go into a room filled with sunshine
but she had dirt in her eyes and could hardly open them. *This
dwelling is actually bright*, but the soul cannot appreciate it because these wild beasts make her close her eyes to everything
but them."[24] This divine light is present from the very beginning, the very ground of our desire to seek in the first place.

Teresa's quirks of character, faults, and failures remain
with her just as they do with each of us. As Teresa lives out
of the flowering of unitive awareness, she is still at the height

of her activity and much in need of her sharp, thinking mind for the practical and practically impossible tasks with which she was faced: founding reformed Carmelite monasteries for both the women and men of her Order; negotiating the worst sorts of political scheming, especially from the resisting male branch of her Order; writing to King Philip II of Spain to ask him to intercede on her behalf; to say nothing of her need to present herself under the guise of a mere woman in order to escape censorship by the male authority of her day. At the same time she can speak out of this unitive awareness of how she perceives things from within.

Teresa's younger protégé and co-reformer, St. John of the Cross (1542–1591), speaks of what takes place in the hiddenness of ourselves unselfed of self, simply saying in *The Living Flame of Love,* "God is your center."[25] In *The Sayings of Light and Love*, he speaks of the simplification of our prayer life: "Preserve a loving awareness of God, with no desire to feel or understand any particular thing about God."[26] But for those who have practiced contemplation for quite some time, the preposition "of" in the phrase, "loving awareness of God" simply falls away. God cannot be an object of awareness, for God would then not be God. John of the Cross not only provides us with a glimpse of what his own practice of contemplation might have been like, but he also attempts to put into words what life looks like to someone in whom the inner eye of unitive awareness has opened up from within awareness. "It seems to such a person . . . that the entire universe is an ocean of love in which one is engulfed; for, conscious of the living center of love within, it is unable to catch sight of the boundaries of this love."[27] No dualisms can navigate the ocean of contemplation. Like all dualisms, they are in the eyes of the dualist.

Another voice in this great choir is that of St. Elizabeth of the Trinity (1880–1906), who lived a mere twenty-six years and who ponders what her role in heaven might be. In one of her many letters she writes, "I think that in heaven my mission will be to keep [people] in this great silence within that will allow God to communicate Himself to them and *transform them into Himself*."[28] St. Elizabeth of the Trinity knows that this silence within is a manifestation of what normal is. The Carmelite saint embodies both the Silence that can't be said as well as this very Silence in mission. Her one goal is to show our own normality.

Two outstanding Jewish writers add their voices to our Song of Union: Edith Stein (St. Benedicta of the Cross) and the saintly Etty Hillesum. Right in the thick of World War II, Edith Stein (1891–1942) is taken from her Carmelite monastery in Echt, The Netherlands, and put on a death train to Auschwitz. The Third Reich has begun to exterminate the Jewish community in Holland. This includes Edith Stein, for even though she converted to Catholicism and became a Carmelite nun, she remained both proud of and in deep solidarity with her Jewish heritage, her loving family, and all the Jewish people and their plight. She would never want to deny any of this even if it led to her extermination at Auschwitz. She prays movingly in *Verses from a Pentecost Novena*: "You are the space that embraces my being and buries it in yourself."[29] Her realization of such divine intimacy accompanies her to Auschwitz. A photograph of her looking out the window of the death train reveals a serene calm as she "beholds the affairs of life" as Evagrius understated it earlier.

A remarkable Jewish writer, Etty Hillesum (1914–1943), is likewise marked for death at Auschwitz. A professed atheist with a sharp, analytical mind, the existence of God, to say nothing of a deep intimacy with God, would not remotely have captured her interest. Completely unbidden, and not especially wanted, Etty begins to notice something stirring within her. She hasn't the foggiest idea what to make of it. Only gradually does she begin to realize that there is a vast presence opening from within her. On June 11, 1941, Etty writes in her diary: "My inner landscape consists of great, wide planes, infinitely wide, with hardly a horizon in sight— one plane merging into the next."[30] In her diary entry on June 21, 1942, she asks herself, "What was it like this morning, just before I woke up? An almost tangible feeling, just as if there were all sorts of spaces and distances locked up inside me which now wanted to break out to unfold into ever wider spaces and distances. . . . Like stamping and pawing horses from a crowded stable. That spatial feeling within me is very strong."[31] It gradually begins to dawn on her that "the inner world is as real as the outer world. . . . It too has its landscapes, contours, possibilities, its boundless regions."[32] Another entry reveals her realization that "It is as if I were riding through the landscape of my own soul. Soul-scape. I feel that often: that the outer landscape is a reflection of the inner."[33]

As gradual as it is unbidden, Etty's realization of this opening up from within a vast "Soul-scape," radiant, sweeping, expansive, leads her to observe that "Thinking gets you nowhere."[34] This comes as a rather startling statement from a fiercely analytical young thinker. She continues, "You shouldn't live on your brains alone but on deeper, more abiding sources, though you should gratefully accept your brains as a precious tool for delving into what problems your soul brings forth."[35] This humbling of the thinking mind serves what our "soul brings forth," the unbidden Soul-scape opening up from within, "expansive and radiant." Her inner realization of this only deepens as she comes to see that the thinking mind alone does not suffice.

This humble and reverent kneeling of the brain before what "the soul brings forth" is not easy for her to take on board. Her difficulty in consenting to rational thought's bending of the knee shows itself in her difficulty in assuming the physical posture of kneeling. She is attracted to the posture of kneeling even as she resists it. In yet another remarkable diary entry, this on September 24, 1941, she writes, "This afternoon I suddenly found myself kneeling on the brown coconut matting in the bathroom, my head hidden in my dressing gown, which was slung over me. I feel sort of embarrassed. Why? Probably because of the critical, rational, atheistic bit that is part of me as well. And yet every so often I have a great urge to kneel down with my face in my hands and in this way to find some peace and to listen to that hidden source with me."[36]

Etty Hillesum's voice is important for us to listen to. She neither requests nor desires what begins to open up from within her. Indeed this rationalist does not know what to make of any of this. Her razor-sharp, analytical mind in fact resists it. Yet somehow she manages to stay out of the way. We who practice with dedication and regularity often fall overboard by trying too hard. Etty teaches contemplatives the importance of staying out of the way. And so we deepen by way of consent, by giving voice to our own small *fiat*, "let it be done according to thy will" (Lk 1:38).

Who sings in her role in the song of union more movingly than the character of Celie in Alice Walker's powerful *The Color Purple*? "Here's the thing, say Shug. The thing I believe. God is inside you and inside *everybody* else. You come into the world with God. But only them that search for it inside find it."[37]

OUR VOICES IN THE CHOIR

"Because I have a voice!" So shouts Colin Firth's stammering King George VI. We ourselves often find it hard to believe that we too have a voice in this choir. But our own voices are likewise voices in this choir whether we realize it or not.

It is common enough for us to say to ourselves, "Well, this choir is all for rarefied saints and doctors of the church, monks or nuns, not for normal people like me who live in the real world." By convincing ourselves of this we degrade what "normal" is. It is not normal for a rosebush not to bloom; it is not normal for an eagle not to soar; it is not normal for crystal not to sparkle as it jostles light. So why should we think it is not normal for us to realize in the days given us that we too "have a voice!" in the very same choir?

In our very singing we gradually realize the fullness of our own creation. The full-flowering of who we are remains forever *hidden* (Col 3:3). This self un-selfed of self can never be seen as an object; nor can it be charted; nor can it enneagram*ed*; nor can it be Myers Briggs*ed*. Helpful as these tools often are, ultimately they are only labels. As R. S. Thomas says to God:

> It begins to appear
> this is not what prayer is about.
> It is the annihilation of difference,

the consciousness of myself in you, of you in me; . . .
Circular as our way
is, it leads not back to that snake-haunted garden. . . .[38]

We do well to remember that each of the voices we have heard finds its place in this choir precisely because it lived some of the very struggles we live. It ultimately realizes what is so precious, so simple—that "God's ground is my ground and my ground is God's ground."[39] Even if it takes our entering the transforming mystery of death to realize that we are light sitting in Light.

The suffering and death of Jesus shaped much of Christian culture both East and West, to say nothing our own lives. Let the Letter to the Hebrews speak for us: "We find in Jesus, someone who is no stranger to our weakness. For he has been tried as we are tried" (Heb 2:18).

Those of us who know suffering all too well—physically, emotionally, or both—find solidarity with St. Paul, who knew intense struggle for a good deal of his life and speaks of his "thorn in the flesh" (2 Cor 12:8ff). Paul is forever asking God to relieve him of this thorn in the flesh (we don't know what it is because Paul quite sensibly does not tell us), but God simply says to Paul, "Your struggles remain. But what you get is me." This transforms Paul's entire relationship with suffering. What had previously been experienced as defeat is now experienced as a vehicle of Presence. Because of this, Paul now delights in his weakness, for he has discovered that Divine Love is attracted to what we loathe most in ourselves (2 Cor 12:8–11).

St. Catherine of Genoa marries a physically abusive (and rather well-off) man, and all the while she keeps to her daily ministry of tending the sick and the orphaned.

St. Teresa of Avila suffers a long illness in her youth. This infirmity proves to be the catalyst of a profound conversion that bore fruit in her reforming both the female and male branches of the Carmelites throughout Spain. She could never have foreseen any of this as she lay suffering. She was on the road much of the time, founding new monasteries, and living the challenges of being a woman in a man's world; her now classic writings were at first held in suspicion and open to censure simply because she was a woman. In obedience to the culture of the time, she regularly put herself down so as to appear but a mere woman who knows nothing in order to stay under the radar of male authority.

St. John of the Cross is treated maliciously by his own confrères and repeatedly imprisoned. Long periods of his life are marked by darkness, rejection, the feeling of never being understood by his community.

St. Edith Stein is born into an observant Jewish family. An atheist by her teenage years, she goes on to become one of the most brilliant philosophers of her day. After her conversion to Catholicism, she suffers the bitter disappointment of the family she both loves and is loved by. In the end, the Nazis put her on the death train for Auschwitz.

Etty Hillesum, also a Jewish atheist as a young adult, lives a tortured life of inner suffering as an emotional self-cutter until, after years of psychoanalysis bears fruit, an inner life begins to stir, which she ultimately calls God, as this Mystery opens ever more deeply within her. A strongly committed social activist, she is yet Jewish and, in solidarity with all those of Jewish heritage, is likewise sent to Auschwitz.

None of these people is spared the sorrows and pain that each of us experiences as we struggle to get through each day. Why is this so? Because our lives don't go as we would have them? As the contemporary French poet Christian Bobin puts it, "We fail our lives. We fail everything. What is strange in fact is that grace still gets to us, when we do all we can to render ourselves unreachable."[40]

"ORPHANS OF LIGHT"

Why are so many of us unaware of this River of Light coursing through each one of us? Throughout the ages there have been many terms used to explain this: the Fall, original sin, originating sin, being born into the human condition, and so on. While some of us may find one or another of these labels helpful, others still carry baggage with some of these terms that we find difficult to let go of. Each of these terms is meant to address the same thing: something that none of us is personally guilty of or responsible for but which we all somehow find to be our common situation. Again Christian Bobin sets this in helpful perspective, "All I have seen in the nobility of self-forgetful faces has been the traces of this radiance towards which each life is tending without knowing it."[41]

For our purpose it might be helpful to view all this through the lens of the practice of contemplation. St. Diodochus of Photike (among many others) provides a useful way of looking at it. For St. Diodochus, unitive awareness is normal for humans: "the perceptive faculty natural to our soul *is single*."[42] He goes on to explain that this single eye is somehow split into dualistic awareness, what he calls a "dislocation which takes place in the mind."[43] The result is that the normal, natural state of perceiving the unity of all things we now experience through a sort of dualistic awareness—the world of this as opposed to that, the Hatfields and the McCoys, the Montagues and the Capulets, the world of imitation and violence, the world of "wars and rumors of war" (Mt 24; Mk 13:4).

The unnatural world of blind and blinding dualisms of true self versus false self, of dual versus non-dual, the sense that we're over here and God is over there needing to be sought and found, as yet one more thing in a long line of other things, somehow this dualistic awareness wins the day.

The result of this is that normal, unitive awareness (unitive awareness has no opposite just as the deep ground of Silence is generous enough to embrace both sound and no sound, and yet manifests itself in both sound and no sound) lies buried and seems undeveloped. The practice of contemplation cultivates the interior ground that allows this inner eye to open up within awareness, *the very aware-ing* itself. This awakens us to our normal state of awareness that perceives the grounding unity of all things.

Until by grace we come home to our normal state where are we left? We are somehow imprisoned by the siren song of the Mercedes, which we can purchase, polish, and watch others watching us. How did this happen? St. Diodochus uses the language most characteristic of his age: "a result of Adam's disobedience."[44] We are free to use other language to describe human alienation from its own normality. As the poet Franz Wright puts it in his poem "Scribbled Testament":

> I stand before you
> here, some hairy
> primate's fall from grace—
> one of the patients of God,
> one of the orphans of light.[45]

Whatever we call it we somehow, to quote Christian Bobin again, "render ourselves unreachable."[46]

St. Diodochos goes on to say that this undivided faculty of unitive awareness becomes normal once again when it is "enlightened by the Holy Spirit in the inner shrine of our heart."[47] It is important to bear in mind that in ancient Jewish and Christian spirituality "the heart" is not the Hallmark card heart with the flappy wings of pinkish baby angels flying about that we're compelled to purchase with real money and send on Valentine's Day. Nor is it the death-dealing dualism of mind versus heart, which seems to be forever stuffed into our mouths, as we say, for example, "in my head I think it's time to sell the house at a profit but in my heart I really don't want to leave this place." Examples of this dualism in action are countless. However, this "stacked up" head–heart split is not what St. Diodochos means when he says "enlightened by the Holy Spirit in the inner shrine of our heart." In Judeo-Christian tradition "heart" intends the unifying, grounding, center of the human person. The heart in this deep sense permits no "stacked up" dualisms, which shape our culture and our lives.[48] Like that old dandelion that's been around for years, it has taken root in the lawns of our lives and is next to impossible to root out. Proper weed that it is, it knows just when to break off, leaving bits of root behind so that it can grow right back in less than a week. Dualisms are always easier to live out of and more difficult to root out. They give us a sense of being in control when in fact we are asleep behind the wheel. More important, that which wants to exterminate all dandelions is itself the weed of dualism. The best way to deal with dualisms of any nature is to sit so still before God that the "before" finally falls away and we are freed up so as to "make stillness the criterion for testing the value of everything, and choose always what contributes to it," as Evagrius advises.[49] Otherwise we are left going through life asleep at the switch. "We are most deeply asleep at the switch," says Annie Dillard, "when we fancy we control any switches at all."[50]

Even if we are yet to recognize our own voice in this Song of Union, it is easy to find ourselves humming along; we are taught it somehow whenever, in a self-forgetful moment, we engage life, however it happens to be at any given time, whether things are going well in our lives or all hell is breaking loose. But we do not need to read or study anything about all this. Simple kitchen wisdom teaches all we need to know. At least this is something the eavesdropper learned.

THE EAVESDROPPER AND THE SOUFFLÉ

"Haven't you ever made a soufflé?" These are the words one woman says to her friend in the local grocery store. A tiresome eavesdropper immediately zeroes in. The second woman (let's call her Sue) responds curtly, "Of course I've made a soufflé. What's that got to do with bringing God into my life?" Sue asks her friend (let's call her Constance), "How do I bring God into my life the way you have done?" Her amused bemusement prompts Constance to ask, "What on earth do you mean? God doesn't need to be brought anywhere. God is already both within and without." The eavesdropper follows this intrigue as the two grocery carts depart fresh produce and enter the maze of boxed cereals. Constance says, "Well, it's all very much like throwing together a soufflé. You've got your soft, stiff peaks of egg whites and you've got your mixture. Sweet or savory, it doesn't matter. But these two are not the one soufflé." "Obviously not," says Sue, rolling her eyes. Constance continues, "Say the silken peaks of egg whites are God and the mixture is ourselves."

By now this conversation has taken the two women, and the eavesdropper, out of the cereal aisle and over into dairy. "Before the mixture is folded into the egg whites, some of the egg whites are stirred into the mixture. This makes it easier for it to be folded into the white peaks. Then it's time to gently fold the mixture into the soft white peaks. So you see, don't you? There is already something of God within the mixture of our life that makes it easier to be folded fully into God."

After this over-spiritualized cooking lesson Sue rolls her eyes again. "Then," Constance continues, "when the mixture has been folded in, you turn out the entire thing into the soufflé dish. The heat of the Holy Spirit brings these two ingredients to completion in the *one* soufflé, which is no longer made up of two separate ingredients. It rises until golden, ready to remove, let sit, and then be served to others. What goes into the oven looks very different from what comes out. But nothing new has been added. The activation by the heat of the Holy Spirit makes it rise with golden dignity and magnificence."

Sue interjects, "You have apparently forgotten that years ago I taught *you* how to make a soufflé. But I had no idea of the spiritual rush you seem to get out of all this. And besides, I'm baking an apple tart for tonight anyway." Constance says with even more enthusiasm, "Apple tart! Oh! This is how you make an apple tart."

The eavesdropper departs this private conversation as discretely as he entered it. He stops after some distance and turns round to observe the two women. Constance stands upright. Sue hunches over.

Sue knows the recipe and technique. She knows the map but not the territory. Constance knows the territory. This allows her to gaze upon broader landscapes while following the very same recipe as Sue. Constance knows the deep places of the simple suchness of right now. She is the more receptive learner of kitchen wisdom, for she is attentive to what kitchen wisdom teaches each day: there is something of God already within us that allows us to be folded into God in fullness. This is precisely what Eriugena, who likewise knows both the map and the territory, said of St. John the Evangelist: "He would not have been able to ascend into God if he had not first become God."[51] Some call this the divine image. The wise say nothing at all.

This is true of each of us, including Dorothy Parker even as she recovers from a great night out. Dorothy Parker herself is said to have mastered her soufflé with the juice of one orange, the zest of one orange, some butter, and Grand Marnier.

PART II

THREE

Distant Echoes of Home

Reactive Mind

Take the plank out of your own eye before you remove the speck
from your neighbor's.
— Matthew 7:5; Luke 6:42

My heart was deafened by the din of my mind.
— St. Augustine

INTRODUCTION

The present moment is our home. In its rooms we discover
the fullness of our common life hidden in eternity. Until our
lives, especially our emotional habits and completely unremarkable daily routines, have been integrated into the mystery of this simplest of facts, we shall more than likely think
that we must make space for God in our lives, so as to invite
God in. But this distorts the relationship and keeps us, as the
poet Franz Wright puts it, "orphans of light."[1] If God is already closer to us than we are to ourselves, as St. Augustine

famously reminds us,[2] or again as Franz Wright echoes St. Augustine:

> Closer to me than my bones you
> you are there[3]

then who are we to invite God in, who is already the very ground of our seeking? *God is the great invitation*—an invitation to release perpetually into that Love which finds Sabbath rest in us and sustains us in being.

Here there is no in or out; no before or after; no above or below; "no Jew or Greek, slave or free, no male or female; for we are all one in Christ Jesus" (Gal 3:28). In the mystery of God in Christ there are no such socially sanctioned distinctions and permissions to exclude; no personal or social permissions for comparison, rivalry, or violence.

There is but an eternal now. The silence of the eternal now is simply Love's embrace shining like the sun, bathing us in that light, "where eternity clips time."[4] Love itself is nothing other than this eternal now. As R. S. Thomas writes:

> . . . love is
> a moment eternally overflowing.[5]

Overflowing as what? The divinizing humanity of Christ enfolding our own humanity into the unfathomable mystery of His Person.

"REMOVE THE PLANK FROM YOUR
OWN EYE"

What is this "true self" or "real self" we hear so much about?

The true self as opposed to the false self is yet another un-helpful dualism that is peddled by many in the spirituality industry who speak of this "false self" as though it were some sort of something to be rid of. If there is anything to be rid of, it is the illusion that there is something that needs to be rid of in the first place, and that there is likewise some separate person who does the ridding. We travel the earth in search of our "true self" and pay sums of money to acquire what cannot be acquired, because by birthright we have always been who we are. And so we drive around town in the very car we think we have lost and must find.

Although we can speak of an unchartable progression in the spiritual life (not promotion or certification), such progress often does not feel much like progress at all. Moreover, there is no place to advance to and no separate subject in need of advancing toward this "no place to advance to" (about which more later). This marks the great, releasing realization: when our practice of contemplation reveals this to us, then we shall have discovered the "pearl of great price" (Mt 13:46). Our identity, our life, call it a "self" if you like (or worse "the self"), *is forever hidden*, "hidden with Christ in God" (Col 3:3). Our created, creative identity flows from and is consummated by the eternal splendor of the ineffable, divinizing humanity of the mystery of God in Christ. The Psalmist expresses the intimacy of this love, "For you created my inmost being; you knit me together in my mother's womb" (Ps 139:13). The prophet Jeremiah likewise speaks of our being intimately known by God before we were even conceived, "before I formed you in the womb I knew you" (Jer 1:5). The echoes of the Psalmist and the prophet are heard and passed on by the anonymous sixteenth-century Flemish author of *The Temple of Our Soul*, who stands on the shoulders of a cloud of witnesses. The soul is filled with light "so that it might know that [God] knew it before it existed, that [God] loved it when it did not yet exist."[6] Paradoxically, when we find ourselves hidden with Christ in God, there is no separate self there to do either the finding or the hiding; such is the overflowing fullness of created identity.

As we shall see, Light comes streaming through both the "false self" and the "true self," including the noise-generated dualisms that reactive mind manages to see everywhere. We go at these dualisms tooth and nail, and dualistically bludgeon them into what we triumphantly label "the non-dual." Reactive mind (indeed receptive mind too) is compelled to label what cannot be labeled. Because our inner eye is so cluttered (Mt 7:5), we miss the simplicity of Light kissing the rib cage of failure. This does not mean our faults and failings disappear, leaving only virtue's splendor. The Light that illumines the whole of our identity in God is at once the luminous ground of our solidarity in communal frailty and failure. Our hiddenness "with Christ in God" (Col 3:3) sustains no separate "me" but a self-forgetful, self-giving "we." Such is the grounding solidarity of all humanity *in conspectu Dei* (in the sight of God). The depth of our solidarity in the life of God in Christ constitutes the foundation of personal integrity. Light streams freely, joyfully, and generously to reveal both our dangerously delusive falsehoods as well as the simple truths of each one of our lives and loves. Yet such liberating insight remains insulated from us by the inner clutter of reactive mind.

St. Augustine has often reminded us that the purpose of the Christian life is the "healing of the eye of the heart whereby God may be seen."[7] What is wrong with this eye of the heart? Let the parable of Jesus respond, as well as set the course for what follows in these chapters: "Take the plank out of your own eye before you remove the speck from your neighbor's eye" (Mt 7:5; Lk 6:42). For St. Augustine, it seems, the purpose of the Christian life is not so much the opening of this inner eye as the healing of an inner eye that is already open but suffers from lumbered vision, mental clutter that occludes the unitive gaze of the eye of the heart. Contemplative practice gradually dispels the illusion of separation from God. Through the medicine of grace, the eye of our heart is healed by the gradual removal of the lumber of mental clutter, "the plank in our eye" that obscures the radiance of the heart. This radiance is a ray of God's own light.

Psalm 139:13 and Jeremiah 1:5 echo down the centuries and are heard by another sixteenth-century Flemish author, who in *The Evangelical Pearl* writes, "Now I give myself once again entirely, . . . as when I was yet uncreated in you."[8] Self-forgetful giving is likened to when we were yet uncreated.

The eye of the heart is awareness itself, light receiving Light; light sitting in Light; Light from Light, as the Nicene Creed puts it—the Father's Light that is likewise the Son's. We cannot be aware of this awareness any more than we can be aware of the "non-dual." We participate so deeply in this awareness as to *be* this very awareness. This is our life together.

Why do we live unaware of our radiant ground? It is a very long story. Classically referred to as the Fall, this way of explaining what we now often call "the human condition" has often been told and frequently interpreted rather badly. With respect to the life of contemplation, which concerns us here, St. Diodochos of Photiki frames it well: "this single faculty of perception is split because of the dislocation which, as a result of Adam's disobedience, takes place in the intellect."[9] What had enabled us to be a unitive gaze that perceived no subject/object opposition but self-forgetful communion now perceives God in shards of broken mirror, both within and without. The unitive gaze of the single eye of the heart is luminous vastness gazing into luminous vastness, the seat of our identity-in-solidarity. However, as St. Diodochos maintains, what we had perceived as unity is now split and is fixed instead on the mental refuse of inner noise that we now take as normal, what St. Augustine calls "the din of my mind." As a result, we view God as an external object to be sought after. Likewise our "true self" is something to go out there and find. The grounding unity is constant, but our vision is both blinded and blinding; fragmented and fragmenting.

We do well to remember that the metaphor of decluttering does not imply a clearly delineated succession of stages; for the clutter of the mind comes and goes and comes again, in a process much like keeping house or trying to keep our desks clear of heaped-up paper and notes. We cannot map what is essentially unchartable. The more the practice of contemplation declutters the mind of reactive and receptive mind, the more the grounding radiance of unitive aware-ness shines through. Its unitive, luminous quality has been present in its fullness since before we were born. The mind cleared of clutter allows the grounding radiance of unitive mind to manifest the fullness that is its essence, both in time and in eternity. Remember the Psalmist and the prophet: "For you created my inmost being; you knit me together in my mother's womb" (Ps 139:13); "Before I formed you in the womb I knew you" (Jer 1:5). God is the knitter for whom there are no dropped stitches; a Presence too simple to be absent and in whom there is no before or after, within or without; a Presence likewise so simple as to manifest as absence, as both before and after, both within and without.

To help us appreciate this radical decluttering let us look at how four themes appear and disappear differently in reactive mind, receptive mind, and luminous mind: What is practice like? What is ego like? What contemplative skills are developing? What are some special challenges? Each of these indices of awareness (there are others) looks different in reactive mind, receptive mind, and luminous mind.

THE LARGE, SMALL
COFFEE: REACTIVE MIND

Matthew, let us call him, lived in Europe for virtually all the 1990s. When he returned home to the United States, just in time for the new millennium, the culture had changed quite a bit. Apart from vague apocalyptic feelings breaking out into a collective "Y2K" panic, the fear that at the stroke of midnight on that New Year's Eve computers around the world would crash, ATM machines would somehow swallow all our money alive, as well as loads of other horrid things that never happened and have long since been forgotten about. Matthew observed many cultural changes, but one of the most jolting ones had to do with coffee.

When Matthew left the country in 1990, there were no such things as coffee bars or SUVs. By the end of that decade there were coffee shops in any direction he looked. They sold you a small coffee that was called "grande" (which of course means "big" or "large"). The SUVs seemed to be outnumbering the soccer-mom minivan which itself had replaced the all-reliable station wagon. SUVs barreled around town, their drivers highly caffeinated by one of those small coffees called a large coffee. The actual large coffee was served in a fortified paper cup that could likewise function as a vase or even a small planter.

Another cultural development was something called "road rage." Matthew could not help but observe a clear connection between the highly caffeinated drivers of SUVs and the sudden eruptions of road rage. If someone else beat the driver of the SUV-caffeine-mobile to the red light (where everyone ended up stopping and waiting anyway), there could be quite an explosion of rage. The caffeine-mobile in question did not have to be an SUV; the rage-response was the same no matter the breed of car. The rage-response of the driver would involve a long and often varied performance on the horn while coming so close to the car in front that it nudged it forward. Matthew once saw such a display of road rage that the driver's car nearly mounted the car in front. Rage-response occasionally resulted in an attempted physical assault.

Reactive mind is characterized by a compulsion to acquire as well as a throttling need to progress toward mastery. It is what we embarrassingly call our normal way of life, shaped by a culture that feeds on compulsion, consumption, conquest, credit, and cash. Reactive mind serves to keep God at bay even as we desire God all the same. Inconsistency and contradictions are its daily bread.

There is a frightened, defensive quality to reactive mind that is always at the ready. It is second nature to us and supported by a heavy momentum that has been generated by a lifetime of going through life merely reacting to what is going on within us and around us. Reactive mind is something like being caught in a phone booth with a bee. In days gone by when we used phone booths, we would enter and close the door. Our coins clinked into the phone. We were focused as we dialed the number. Then suddenly we notice that there is a bee in the phone booth with us. Our consciousness immediately splits off like billiard balls clacking off in all directions. We begin to bob and weave as our bodies slam first against one side of the booth, then the others; suddenly we are crouched down trying desperately to avoid something that is desperately trying to avoid us. This bee-in-the-phone-booth performance typifies reactive life and awareness, and it is so second nature that we think this is what normal is.

What Is Practice Like?

James (let us call him) proves a good example of what contemplative practice looks like in reactive mind. James is remarkably well read in spirituality (as well as in politics, economics, and community organization) and he is very quick to let you know it. The mere mention of any book is greeted by the nodding of his head, as if to say: "Yes, I've read that and know all about it." James does this even if it is the first time he has ever heard of the book. Nor is he aware that his strong attraction to spirituality and spiritual practices is the very measure of his distancing himself from these very things. He takes refuge in spirituality the way Adam took refuge behind a bush when Yahweh was passing by (Gen 3:8).

James comes from a large family with more than its fair share of dysfunction as a consequence of fame, fortune, and misfortune. His loving parents are themselves driven, and in turn they drove their children to be super-achievers, to make something of themselves. James and his siblings do indeed achieve and make something of themselves, but in the process *they never became themselves*.

Like most of us, James turns around and is suddenly an adult. But in adulthood all of that drive to succeed and achieve suddenly becomes life-pain and the source of as much grace as disgrace. His tucked-away sense of abandonment *fuels* his compensating need to perform to anxious perfection; yet perfection is never quite good enough. He is highly competitive, yet must always have the approval of all, with the result that he runs with the foxes and hunts with the hounds. James has mastered the language of family-systems analysis just to let you know that he both knows all about the ghosts from his personal history and has expelled them all. In fact, he has never really dealt with any of this but he does *know* it is there. However, a pervasive sense of emotional abandonment accompanies him in adulthood. He keeps all this closely under wraps and never looks it in the eye. Yet it remains there, just on the periphery of his vision.

Still deeper is his desire for God that has been with him all his life. Genuine as this desire is, all his pretty talk about spirituality is actually aesthetic distancing: the attraction to something beautiful or alluring (such as life with God) is used as a defense against that deep self-knowledge which ultimately leads to knowledge of God.[10]

What is James's practice like? It's all over the place. But he is able to sit still. It's actually very inspiring the way he sits perfectly still for the duration of 30 minutes in the early hours of the morning, well before he has to get ready to go to work. Indeed his body is in stillness. That is, once he gets himself to the chair he uses for prayer. Getting to the chair is another matter altogether.

He has an arsenal of procrastination techniques to defend himself against doing what he desires most to do: to be still in the presence of the Lord (Ps 46:10). Therefore, first the trash has to be taken out it's 5:00 a.m, which won't be collected before 8:00 a.m. Then it's straight to prayer. But then he's got to wipe down the countertops, which he had already wiped down the night before just so he wouldn't have to wipe them down when he got up early in the morning to pray. Now that the countertops are clean (again), it's straight to prayer. But there might be some emails to delete. That's done. He glances at his cell phone and there's a text that requires immediate attention (it's 5:30 a.m.!). That's done. Now it's time to pray. Oops, Amazon! A new history of spirituality can now be one-clicked (as though it couldn't be done 30 minutes later). Done. Now time to pray. But there might be some emails that arrived in the last five minutes. Quick check. Nope. Facebook! It's now 6:30 a.m., but finally he's there. His body-mind is a beehive of activity.

What is our practice like when the mind's whisk is constantly frothing up reactive mind? Because we each have different minds, no two of us will have exactly the same experience. Nevertheless, there are some common elements. Throughout the years of practice, the basics remain basically the same: whenever we find that our attention has been stolen by a thought, feeling, or image (it is all the same cognitive stuff), we bring the attention back to our prayer-word united with the breath. St. John Climacus (sixth century) famously put it, "Let the name of Jesus cling to your every breath and you will know the meaning of silence."[11] While some form of the Jesus Prayer is obviously intended here, there are other contemplative practices that likewise serve to cultivate both the power of inner concentration and the expansion of awareness (the two are one) so as to reveal the fathomless depths of the interior silence that has always been present. Many of us change our practice somewhat frequently for a variety of reasons—often just because things get a bit boring. But as a general rule of thumb we want to avoid frequently changing our prayer-word, *especially* when our current practice has grown boring. We do well to recall that boredom is often the work of grace within our practice and a sign of crucial deepening beyond what our senses can grasp. Since God cannot be grasped in the way perceptible objects can, boredom serves to wean us away from equating union with God and feelings of God's presence as a state of constant peace and recollection. These feelings are impermanent, patterns of weather but not the mountain itself.

Changing our practice often does not allow our practice to put down roots deeply into the soil of the present moment. Over time, changes will take place, but these changes are due to the developmental dynamic intrinsic to practice itself. It's the sort of change that takes place when we plant a rosebush. The energy that enables the rosebush to put down roots is the same energy that enables the production of stems, leaves, buds, and flowers. Yet if we were to dig up the rosebush several times and replant it, telling ourselves, "The light is better over here." A week later, "No it's better over there." Two weeks later, "Wait! There's better drainage over there with the other roses." A few weeks later, "Oh for God's sake, those rosebushes get black spot and powdery mildew. I should transplant them all." The more this sort of thing goes on, the less we can expect from our roses. The rosebush needs stability, sun, soil, and water to draw forth the life already within it.

The practice of contemplation is not an attempt to have no thoughts. This only serves to build up tension in the body and keep us forever checking to see if we're having any thoughts. This in turn increases the momentum of reactive mind and the lifestyles born of it (their numbers are legion). The practice is returning and returning and returning, *without* a speck of any expectation of results (mercifully, results are often kept out of our sight; otherwise we would be forever journaling about them). Practice gradually trains the attention and grounds us more solidly in our bodies, increasing our ability to be where our bodies are at any given moment.

When reactive mind dominates, bringing the attention home to our practice is more challenging that it sounds. We may think we are faithfully returning to our practice. This is certainly our intention, but in fact we are returning to a *buffer of thought* between "us," who sit here practicing a "practice" just there at the other end of our attention.

This buffer of thought is subtle indeed. It is like bringing together the ends of two magnets of the same charge. The two ends will not unite. Take two of the magnets you use on the fridge to hold up various to-do lists and drawings by children and grandchildren. Try to bring the two magnets together. They won't come together because they have the same charge, positive–positive (or north–north). The closer the two ends of the magnet come together the stronger they resist each other. Such is the effect this buffer of thought has on our attention's ability to be one with our practice. This buffer of thought maintains and strengthens our inner resistance to stillness. The advice remains the same: we keep with our practice. This buffer of thought eventually thins. Returning to our practice over and again (now second nature to us), without paying attention to our incessant expectation to acquire anything at all, begins to wear away this buffer of thought in such a way that we are increasingly one with our practice, like magnets of opposite charge (north–south). This buffer of thought suddenly has no illusory, permanent substance. This does not typically happen in reactive mind except perhaps in brief tremors of a moment that don't even register on the Richter scale. When we practice in reactive mind it is more often similar to what the famous monk of Mount Sinai, St. Hesychios (eighth or ninth century) observed: "As soon as a thought appears in our minds we chase after it and become embroiled in it."[12]

With the gradual wearing away of this buffer of thought, the buzzing, compulsive stories in our heads about how our lives and loves should be at any given moment begin to loosen the grip of their narrative. Reactive mind is significantly decluttered of mental refuse. This allows for expansion of receptive mind to begin (life outside the phone booth).

What Is Ego Like?

In reactive mind, ego comes in one size only: Extra-Large. At least this is how reactive mind magnifies and distorts the proper functioning of ego. We might say that ego is the software of reactive mind, so in sync are they. It is important to distinguish "ego," in the sense that concerns us here, from the way it can be used in psychotherapeutic contexts, where the ego needs to be strong enough for the overall psychological functioning, appropriate defenses, psychological boundaries, and self-esteem, among other things. Nor is it some sort of separate entity within us called "ego" that we get rid of while we are busy trying to saw off the dreaded "false self." For our purposes we can describe ego as a sort of knot of psyche. This knot of ego gets in the way of our realizing with expanding clarity that there is no separate, isolated self to begin with, for we are all one in God and always have been. The problem is the knot, not the psychic energy itself. The practice of contemplation does not try to be rid of this knot (this just provides ego with another opportunity to be the center of attention), so much as it allows this knot to loosen up. Gradually the knot loosens its grip on fear, anger, and aggression. Over time this allows psychic energy to flow more smoothly.

In the practice of contemplation, the ego of reactive mind has an astonishing array of maneuvers to keep tautly drawn its knot of separate identity—parasitic and impermanent as it is. Prominent among these are (1) clinging and (2) comparing ourselves with others. Alone and in concert, such maneuvers help maintain ego's domineering, fear-driven need to protect and preserve its tight grip on its sense of being a separate, isolated self.

Clinging

Ego clings to what it wants and discards what it does not want, rather like a child in a pram who safeguards its fiefdom of toys placed there to keep it occupied. Suddenly the child spots the ice cream truck and points demandingly for ice cream RIGHT NOW! The parents say, "Not now, lovey. We haven't had our lunch yet." Upon hearing this, the child lets loose a scream that would wake the dead and begins to throw all its toys out of the pram. It's quite a dramatic tantrum. The usually reliable pacifier is produced and offered. It is immediately hurled out of the pram and rolls under the ice cream truck. It matters not what ego desires or rejects. It operates equally well in a range of reactions varying from high drama to calculating stealth.

Comparing Ourselves with Others

Clinging and rejecting keep reactive ego very pleased with itself. Once ego becomes accustomed to this dreadful practice of contemplation and sees that it is being starved of attention, it adapts itself brilliantly by learning very quickly that it can *imitate* not clinging and letting be. Ego often does this by informing others (anyone at all) but mostly itself how important it is not to cling or reject but "to let be." This serves only to maintain the tautness of the knot of ego's isolated and independent identity. It says to itself, while speaking to others, "That's right. Don't cling. Just let go and let be. Live *into* the path." In order to pull this off smoothly, the ego of reactive mind becomes the master of self-comparison. Typically, when we think no one else is looking, we manage to assess what we have decided someone else's level of spiritual advancement must be (as though there were somewhere else to advance to, something else to acquire). Due to the parasitic nature of reactive ego, we must compare ourselves with others frequently so as to maintain an engorged, thoroughly derived sense of identity. The ego of reactive mind functions rather well in this hall of mirrors, the grandest room in this house of cards. Here we gain complete mastery of all the latest spiritual lingo. The ego of reactive mind really needs to know how well it is progressing on the spiritual path so it can then compare its progress with someone else's. It does not actually need to know the truth of another's progress. But it does need to think it knows.

The greatest of the fourteenth-century Flemish masters, Jan van Ruusbroec, warns us that "We should not dare to compare ourselves with anyone." To counter this mental habit he suggests something that sounds a bit shocking: "rather consider ourselves despicable and unworthy among all people."[13] His advice has nothing to do with cultivating what we would now call low self-esteem. Ruusbroec has something far subtler in mind. He suggests a spiritual practice of sorts to help us counter the firmly entrenched, egoic habit of comparing ourselves with others. These comparisons sustain a sort of rivalry that is self-perpetuating and leads to competiveness. Ruusbroec advises us not to look at others as rivals, but instead to turn our attention to our own faults and failings. This deflates reactive ego, at least for the moment, and breaks the mental habit of comparing ourselves with others. This will lead us to be bathed in the splendor of Divine love, which is somehow attracted to human fault and failing, simply because this is where we are most poor and in need. "For the sake of Christ, then, I am content with weaknesses" (2 Cor 12:10). This new mental habit gradually disposes us to the wellspring of grace within each of us, instead of comparing ourselves with some, usually illusory, standard external to us.

This allows grace to loosen this ego-knot and opens the way to a more expansive, receptive, far less cluttered awareness.

Reactive mind, where this ego-knot is most tightly drawn, is not well schooled in such contemplative skills as "not clinging" or "letting be." Reactive mind looks around at others and decides that, however they are, we must be better.

In reactive mind, "clinging" and "rejecting" seem to be two separate things when in fact they are two sides of a coin. One side of this ego-coin says, "cling to what we like." Turn it over and it says, "reject what you do not like." It is the same knotted awareness and serves the same constricting purpose: ego generates the illusion of separation. Christian Bobin observes, "The living are few and the dead abound in this life—the dead being those who never let go and can't walk away from themselves into love or laughter."[14]

We cannot properly refer to ego as a "self," for ego has no center to live out of and therefore cannot be at one with itself in community. For this reason it is fundamentally parasitic. It draws its life from two things: comparing itself with others and being the center of attention. In fact, it learns its most useful lessons in comparing itself with others when it is the center of attention. This is its illusion-rich nourishment. The purpose of Ruusbroec's teaching on non-comparison is to pull the rug out from under reactive ego's feet (at least for the moment). Because of ego's parasitic nature we must compare ourselves with others so that we can, in turn, imitate them. We derive our sense of who we are from what we think other people think of us. This is why ego can only think in group-think and speak only in group-speak. The danger here is that this derived identity through comparison allows us to establish rivalrous relationships that open the doorway to violence, whether on a small scale or on far grander ones.

Ego is too balled up and frightened to receive, much less be aware of, not only the fact that the receptive, luminous depths of identity require a community but also the realization that, as Franz Wright puts it, "no one is a stranger, this whole world is your home."[15] Christian Bobin likewise expresses what reactive ego can neither see nor express: "A day comes when no one is a stranger to you anymore. That terrible day marks your entry into real life."[16]

We can just begin to see how contemplative practice gently loosens the knot of ego and calms the spasms of reactive mind. When we return our attention to our practice as soon as we are aware that our attention has been stolen, ego is less and less the focus of our attention. The television screen in our heads will continue its constant stream of noise and images. The more we watch and listen to it the duller we feel, a dullness we take to be normal. We grow bored with constantly flipping through channels in search of something that might, one of these rounds, land on something that gives us a sense of being alive instead of being deadened by the din of our minds. The practical answer is simple: let the television play. Simply don't watch it. Gradually (neither in a day nor in a short while) the light of awareness begins to shine through this mental clutter and we begin to realize that the derived identity provided by ego no longer has the ring of truth. "We need to guard," Bobin says, "not only against the world, but against our preoccupation with ourselves, another door by which the world might creep back into us like a prowler into a sleeping house."[17] As the poet David Whyte may well have said of ego, it appears in

> the tangled part of life that refuses
> to be set straight.[18]

Bandaged by the practice of contemplation, reactive ego is no longer as we once lived, loved, and thought. Instead we begin to hear the distant echoes of home, a truth-tolling bell from within.

What Contemplative Skills Begin to Develop?

Cluttered as reactive mind is, certain contemplative skills begin to emerge from our practice to help dislodge the clutter of the mind. We shall focus primarily on two of these skills: the cultivation of a *habitus* and of inner vigilance.

Habitus

The word "habit" sometimes carries the negative connotation of doing something without giving it much thought or out of mere routine such as, "I go to that grocery store just out of habit even though the one further down the road has better produce." Or "I put something in the collection plate just out of habit. Come to think of it, I'd rather not. The sermons are irreverently pious." But "habit" can also mean something very positive such as, "I make a habit of exercising every day." In theology the term "habit" has a technical meaning, which is why it might be better to keep the word in Latin in order to distinguish it from its use in everyday speech. A *habitus* is a dynamism—mental, physical, or moral—that generates an increasingly positive momentum toward love of God and neighbor (this is but one love loving love). There can also be a negative *habitus*, that is, away from love of God and neighbor, but here we shall focus on the positive.

In the practice of contemplation, we see the cultivation of a *habitus* in at least two ways. First, we find 25 to 30 minutes (at least once) each day simply to be the stillness we already are. Generally speaking most find the morning to be the easiest time of the day to reclaim for the purpose of silent prayer. Some use part of their lunch break to find a quiet place. Others find the evening easier. Sometimes we have to be creative about it. Mind you, we don't have to be doing any of this to begin with. The presumption is that we feel some sort of inner drawing toward this; a longing; a sense that this is our path somehow. Typically the first great motivator on this pathless path is the sense that this appeals strongly to something within us. The other great motivator is despair. There are times in our lives, sometimes lasting rather a long while, when just being silent and still is the *least painful* thing we can manage right now, when all our effort is crushed into barely surviving, just keeping one nostril above water. After discovering that pain itself has a silent center and that our own pain is not private to us, however deeply personal it is, something opens up from within, especially if we are too poor to desire that any such opening should ever happen (but we cannot make ourselves poor in order to make this happen).

What brings us to the practice of contemplation does not matter. What matters is that we give ourselves to this practice at least once a day, whether our lives are sunshine or whether all hell is breaking loose (obviously sometimes we will be unavoidably thrown off our routine). At some moment when we are not looking, quantity of time given over to practice will become—without our trying to make it so—quality of time. Suddenly it is second nature to us, and we are beginning to generate (often in just several weeks) a *habitus* that raises the sails to harness the winds of grace. If we only give ourselves to practice once a week or if we wake up one morning and say to ourselves, "It would really be awesome to meditate," this simply isn't enough to establish the momentum of a *habitus*. It would be like eating a vegetable once a week and saying that we are health conscious or taking a walk around the block a few times a month and telling our friends that we like keeping fit. In neither case is something better than nothing. There is not enough quantity to turn into quality; no water to turn into wine (Jn 2:1–12).

The *habitus* will begin to clear away enough of the mental clutter (Mt 7:5) that we can begin to work into our practice the ancient art of vigilance or awareness. It will sound much easier than it is because of the buffer of thoughts generated by reactive mind, but the cultivation of inner awareness is vital.

Vigilant Awareness

The fourth-century desert monk and talented shrink Evagrius of Pontus teaches the practicalities of interior vigilance or awareness (we use these two words interchangeably). The power of concentration that begins to gain the positive momentum of a *habitus* is not separate from the expansion of our awareness. They are two sides of the same coin. Drop a coin into a pool of water and notice that the coin's concentrated plop is inseparable from the expanding ripples of awareness.

In one of his important training manuals, *The Praktikos*, Evagrius says, "We must take care to recognize the different types of demons [afflictive thoughts] and take note of the circumstances of their coming. . . . We ought to consider which of the demons are less frequent in their assaults, which are the more vexatious, which are the ones which yield the field more readily, and which the more resistant."[19] Evagrius is an astute observer of the workings of the mind, and fourth-century psychology of spiritual conflict is expressed in language that features the demons. For purposes of our contemplative training, what is important is the weaponry of the demons: afflictive thoughts (in Greek, *logismoi*). Note that Evagrius is not saying, "Don't have these thoughts." He builds his teaching on the presumption that, just like every other person in history, we struggle with afflictive thoughts. The presence of distracting thoughts is a given, whether they be afflictive, exciting, mundane, completely mad, or utterly silly (like singing to ourselves jingly tunes from our childhood).

Evagrius wants to teach us to change our relationship with thoughts and to discover the true nature of such thoughts. *He does not want to teach us how to get rid of them.* He teaches us how to recognize these distracting thoughts as they occur, as well as what conditions set them off. He wants us to know whether the thoughts come one at a time or team up, and which afflictive thoughts are especially challenging for us. If we only know reactive mind, this sounds more difficult than it actually is. Reactive mind always feels on the defensive against what it takes to be bombardment by thoughts that seem to appear out of thin air. Reactive mind has no choice but to react and cast them aside. Moreover, reactive mind also thinks it has been taught to blank the mind. Lots of luck. The thought, "I have to blank my mind of all thoughts" is just another thought. Reactive mind does not so much identify thoughts as *identify with* thoughts as they come out of seemingly nowhere. Evagrius means to change our identification with thoughts (I am my thoughts) to allowing thoughts simply to be what they are. Just thoughts. A variety of weather patterns occurring on Mt. Zion. But, again, we are neither the storms nor the sunshine of thoughts. We are Mt. Zion, the silent, receptive witness to all weather that comes and goes. Mt. Zion never thinks it is the weather.

We react before we are even aware that we are in a passive mode of reacting to thoughts, a story we tell ourselves. This inner narrative seems to be immediate when it occurs in the clutter or reactive mind. Without being aware of it, reactive mind attaches a story *about* the afflictive thought. The most derailing of these stories are the most subtle and swift.

In fact reactive mind does not even experience the thought-feeling. It experiences only the ego-protecting story about the thought-feeling. Reactive mind is only aware of what is in fact a mask of story that disguises the far simpler thought-feeling, a thought or feeling that is actually naked of all narrative. An afflictive thought, virtually any thought occurring in reactive mind, sets off a cycle of inner chatter that leaves us talking to ourselves—even while we are speaking to others. This inner chatter sustains the illusory, utterly convincing buffer of thought, which itself is the fabrication of reactive mind. This buffer of thought prevents our being one with our practice and convinces us that there is some separate "I" sitting here practicing a separate contemplative practice over there, just at the end of our concentration. This is a prison. Reactive mind would be resigned to live in this prison, insulated from the simple suchness of life and love were it not for the fact that creation bestows an instinctual orientation toward our ground in the grounding love of God. But what if we aren't content to live in a prison? What if our divinely implanted longing for divine union, truth, or wisdom calls the human spirit beyond these comfortable confines of an easily predicted and highly scripted life?

Pop psychology tells us to "feel our feelings." Well said. But pop psychology does not realize that we are not actually feeling our feelings. We may think we are feeling our feelings but what we actually feel is the story we tell ourselves about our thoughts and feelings. We do not feel simple fear. We feel the story *about* what we are afraid of, the story *about* what we are angry at. We are not actually encountering directly the simple thought-feeling naked of narrative, be it pleasant or afflictive. Instead we meet this buffer of thought, a buffer of inner chatter *about* this thought-feeling. This inner chatter, whether tragic or comic, despite its many hats, masks, and wigs, creates and sustains the buffer of thought, "the plank in your own eye." This buffer obscures by its clutter the radiance of awareness, in which both life and death appear and disappear. The sun only knows how to shine. No matter the thickness of the fog the sun yet shines. In his poem "The New Jerusalem," Franz Wright says

> And I knew again, for the millionth time, knew—
> lying all alone there in the dark—you
> can shut both your eyes
> (you can pluck out your eyes), the light
> will still be there[20]

The practical genius of Evagrius eventually steers our attention away from its fixation on inner chatter. We do this by becoming aware of the specific thoughts we are having as they arise, as well as the circumstance that set them off. This does not mean we then start thinking about the thoughts. These are just more stories. For example, we look into the neighbor's driveway. Suddenly there is a knot in our stomach at the sight of their new, top-of-the-line, most expensive Mercedes, not that silly, entry-level Mercedes they bought their kid. We are aware of the knot, but do not even notice the collision of inner commentaries on the fact that the neighbors have purchased the latest, most expensive Mercedes on the market. The collision of thoughts in our head arises seemingly at once: "They're probably only leasing it." "Who would get a Mercedes in *that* color?" "I want a Mercedes!" "I want it in that *very same* color!"

Many other thoughts like this take place completely unnoticed. So we go back inside the house and yell at the children.

Our heads have become a bumper-car rink, with several colliding commentaries. First, there is the entrenched, mental habit of comparing ourselves with others and drawing a conclusion based on this comparison. There is the story of our envy and rivalry because our neighbor has something we think we should have but cannot afford. Attached to this, not following it, is a sense of shame for being an inadequate provider for the family (although we would be the only one allowed to drive the Mercedes). In this case the measure of adequacy is ownership. There is the additional story that we are embarrassed to admit: that we are so caught up in all this to begin with.

Evagrius could not care less about the Mercedes (or the fourth-century camel equivalent). He simply wants us to be able to identify, *as it is happening*, the simple act of comparing ourselves with others, the simple envy, the simple shame, instead of bouncing off the obsessive inner stories *about* the envy, *about* the feeling of being inadequate, etc. In order to recognize which afflictive thought or thoughts are present, we have to be able to shift our attention from the story we are telling ourselves to the simple thought-feeling itself, before the mind whisks it into a story. Not only do we need to see the afflictive thought naked of noise and narrative, we need to know which afflictive thoughts we are prone to and which are not that much of a problem for us; or when they do occur, which "yield the field more readily." We each have different minds and personal histories; what might be life-long struggle for one is not necessarily a problem for another. What is crucial is that we come to know in detail the terrain of our afflictive thoughts and the circumstances that tend to set them off. This will register in reactive mind as being aware of the story but with little sense of any distinction between the simple feeling and the story we tell about it, and what circumstances set it off. There is simply too much clutter to do this as we sit in stillness.

Evagrius teaches, "Now it is essential to understand these matters so that when these various afflictive thoughts set their own proper forces to work we are in a position to address effective words against them, that is to say, those words which correctly characterize the one present. And we must do this before they drive us out of our own state of mind."[21] Another way of getting our attention out of the inner story we tell about the afflictive thought is simply to say without remark or judgment what the afflictive thought is: "Oh, that's greed," "That's fear," "This is my depression talking," and so on. This practice will gradually disentangle our attention from inner chatter, lower its volume, and weaken the throttling grip of these chatter-driven stories. The practice of inner vigilance allows awareness to expand from its normal, knee-jerk, reactive commentary to something that is calmer, more alert, and more receptive than reactive. If we don't learn to do this, Evagrius says, we'll lose our minds.[22]

Early on in our practice, still freighted with reactive mind, the cultivation of inner vigilance might seem to be a lot of work, because the thought-feeling and the story about it seem to be a solid mass. However, when our practice of contemplation establishes its own proper *habitus*, our simple, unselfconscious returning to our practice disentangles awareness from all the clutter. When we are aware that our attention to our practice has been stolen, we bring it back. Returning to our practice and inner vigilance may appear to be two separate things in reactive mind. But in fact these two are one. This becomes more obvious in receptive mind.

Both the cultivation of a *habitus* and the beginnings of our practice of vigilance are skills that begin to develop once our practice is well established. These skills, each a different manifestation of inner silence, will continue to clear away clutter to reveal a brilliance now only dimly lit.

Evagrius's teaching on the cultivation of vigilance produces good fruit. First, we learn to get our attention out of the stories going on in our heads. Second, it introduces us to a glimpse of the inner spaciousness that is silence. Third, this yields growth in self-knowledge. Fourth, self-knowledge becomes less a matter of knowing about ourselves than a falling away of self, a self unselfed of self, and therefore one with all in the intimate love of God, who has sought and found us from all eternity.

The Mercedes? It doesn't even belong to the man next door. It belongs to his brother. The neighbor drove his brother to the airport in the Mercedes and will collect his brother in it in a few days. So there are not any Joneses there to keep up with in the first place, just presumption and spasms of rivalrous envy.

Special Challenges

What are some of the special challenges that typify the practice of contemplation when dominated by reactive mind? There are many. Let us focus on the following: (1) fidelity to practice; (2) the buffer of thought; (3) aesthetic distancing; (4) imitating others.

Fidelity to Practice

This sounds too obvious to need stating. Fidelity to daily (or as close to daily as possible) practice is essential, and presumably there is a sustaining desire to do so. Yes, there will be changes in the weather of desire. But such winds are good for us. A tree cannot stand upright unless it has met the resistance of wind. Somehow we keep showing up no matter what it feels like to sit in stillness at any given moment. When reactive mind begins to soften its grip on the keys to the car, there is often a reactive response, what some have called ego backlash.

Reactive mind does not take any of this lying down. Make no mistake. The ego of reactive mind wrings its hands with delight at the thought of others admiring it for taking on the discipline of contemplative practice. It is all part of its self-protection of deceiving itself by deceiving others. The ego of reactive mind actually feels abandoned and threatened by silence. However, silence is too simple to pose a threat to anything or anybody. This is precisely the problem. Silence gives ego nothing to cling to or to repel from. We can neither cling to silence nor toss it aside—there is nothing there to cling to or toss aside in the first place, so simple is silence. Nor is silence ever separate from anything. When reactive mind dominates the practice of contemplation, it is common enough for us to feel threatened by the simplifying nature of silence. The reaction can be strong, sometimes so strong that even to approach our time and place of prayer is to face into gale-force headwinds. As for sitting still for 25 to 30 minutes: the desire to get up and leave can seem to have the pull of gravity itself, as if the floor has suddenly tilted to a 75-degree angle, like the deck of a ship about to capsize. It takes all our resolve just to remain there and not slide right out the door, fingernails scratching the floor all the way, so strong can the resistance be to what we long for most. And then, the next time we sit in stillness, the wind fills the sails of our practice and we are drawn out into new depths only half-discovered. It is fruitless to predict the patterns of our inner weather.

This is one of the countless paradoxes of the spiritual path: what we alone can do, we cannot do alone. What God has started without us, God does not complete without us. Again, as St. Augustine put it, "So while God made you without you, he doesn't justify without you."[23] We need "a strong hand and an outstretched arm" (Ps 136:12)—what Christians call "grace": the intimate mystery who only gives, "even as we make our lives unreachable," as Bobin has said.[24] Among the fruits of receiving grace is the expansion of our ability to receive. The ability to receive draws us out onto open fields where we are exposed to the vulnerabilities of freedom, where both receiving and giving are a single, self-forgetful exchange.

Buffer of Thoughts

We have spoken of the buffer of thoughts that bestows a subtle—and thus all the more illusory and convincing—sense that there is an "I" sitting here who is faithfully engaged in a contemplative practice somewhere just over there on the other end of our attention.

This buffer of thought remains a special challenge throughout the many seasons when the radiant, groundless ground of being seems overlaid by the mental clutter of reactive mind. Please keep in mind that this groundless ground never loses its luminous vastness. As St. Teresa of Avila bracingly reminds us, despite our faults and at times serious failings, "This fountainhead that shines like the sun from the center of the soul never loses its radiance. It is ever-present within the soul and nothing can diminish its beauty."[25] It is only our mental clutter, grievous errors, or deliberate missteps that prevent our realizing that we are this. It is as though, Teresa continues, a black cloth has been thrown over this radiance, which remains even as we remain unconvinced of it.[26] This will continue until reactive mind has been sufficiently decluttered to reveal our more spacious receptive mind. But to reactive mind, the mere suggestion that there exists this buffer will set it going at it tooth and nail. However, reactive mind only operates out of suggestion, presumption, and insinuation, and cannot actually perceive this buffer of thought. Such is the effect of all our mental clutter. Reactive mind maintains frustration and anxiety in our body-mind and increases the difficulty of something so utterly simple as sitting still.

Aesthetic Distancing

Aesthetic distancing is a subtle, unconscious way of sabotaging our attraction to the beauty of contemplation and the spiritual life, in order to insulate ourselves from the things the contemplative life will make us face head on. Instead, the inherent attraction and beauty of the contemplative life is used as a line of defense in order to keep God at bay. This functions to shield us from the necessary, liberating pains of mental decluttering, which would otherwise contribute greatly to parting the veil of illusion that we are separate from God. Aesthetic distancing subtly co-opts beauty and attraction for egoic purposes, with the result that we subtly reinforce a sense of distance from God. Aesthetic distancing is a challenge like few others simply because it is so hidden, subtle, and attractive. Because it remains for quite some time on the periphery of awareness, it is difficult for our inner vigilance to spot it and stare it down.

A skilled listener can spot us doing this. If asked about our practice, we will exhibit an exaggerated interest or devotion to it and to anything at all to do with our practice. The slightly exaggerated quality of it all is often the tip-off. Devotion can certainly play a positive role in the practice of contemplation, but it differs from the silence of simple *reverence*. In the context of contemplative practice, devotion just gives something else to hold on to, and hence something for grace to rid us of. Let us say, for example, that the prayer phrase is "Sacred Heart of Jesus have mercy. Have mercy." There is *nothing wrong* with this venerable devotion to the Sacred Heart of Jesus, whose liturgical feast (a solemnity) has been celebrated by Roman Catholics since at least 1670. The feast is meant to remind us that the fullness of Jesus' humanity is not some separate thing from the fullness of Divine love. The Sacred Heart wants to draw us into the mystery that these two loves are one love (Jn 10:30; Jn 17:21). All this has its place. However, these insights, thoughts, and devotions have no place during the time of practice—not because they are bereft of meaning that can support our dedication, but simply because they are thoughts. During the time of practice itself (formal or informal), they serve to maintain the perceived distance that we need to be rid of in order to realize ever more deeply the abundance of God's love that comes to us in the humanity of Christ. But reactive ego avoids devotion by clinging to *devotionalism*. This is precisely why the fourteenth-century English author of *The Cloud of Unknowing* exhorts us not to think about the meaning of the prayer-word, "And if, in its great learning, it [the prayer-word] offers to expound that word and tell you its attributes, say that you wish to have it quite whole, and not analysed or explained. . . . And Why? Because you will not let it gratify itself with sweet meditations such as those mentioned earlier."[27] The subtleties of dedicated practice awaken us to the reality that runs deeper than our devotional thoughts and feelings about them can reach. Our thoughts and feelings do not go as deeply as we do, depthless depths that call forth the silent awe of reverence in place of devotion. "Deep calls unto deep in the roar of your waters" (Ps 42:7).

Another sign of aesthetic distancing is that the person feels *routinely* "called" to change the prayer-word. They wore the old one out; they squeezed all the juice out of its personal meaning and (especially) divine inspiration by thinking far too much about its personal meaning for them. As we have said, a contemplative practice is something like a plant. If we are frequently digging up and replanting the plant elsewhere, it will not put down roots.

Another sign, especially if strengthened by the syrup of devotionalism (as distinct from the simplicity of devotion), is a lack of self-knowledge and an abundance of intransigent opinions on just about every spiritual topic that one can possibly invent. The mind has not begun to be decluttered by silence, nor has the ego been bruised by fall and failure—the broom of grace that sweeps clutter away. Perhaps the most obvious sign of the snare of aesthetic distancing is the mastery of spiritual language.

Lacking self-knowledge, we look for ways to convince others, as well as ourselves, of our own spiritual progress. This game maintains our illusion of control over life, love, and pain. We read every spiritual book we can get our hands on in search of sound-bite quotes that we take to be our own. And our mastery of the latest lingo going around the spirituality loop is deployed to convince ourselves and others of all the progress we have attained. *But in fact there is nothing to attain.*

Imitating Others

Aesthetic distancing is closely tied to imitating others. This is another strategy of self-deception to keep both self-knowledge and God at a safe distance. Evagrius warns of the dangers of looking around at others in his *Chapters on Prayer*: "If your spirit still looks around at the time of prayer, then it does not truly pray."[28] Earlier we heard Ruusbroec say even more sternly: "We should not dare to compare ourselves with anyone."[29] Imitating others very quickly leads to rivalry.

We have considered various aspects of the contemplative path through the lens of reactive mind: What is practice like? What is ego like? What contemplative skills begin to develop? What are some special challenges? In the following section we shall consider the very same themes but through the lens of receptive mind. Each of these themes looks different depending on how much mental clutter has been cleared away by the practice of contemplation so as to enable receptive mind to emerge.

We do well not to think of the change of focus from reactive mind to receptive mind as a progression to a different stage in the spiritual life. While the language of stages in the spiritual life is ancient and esteemed, it gives the impression that such stages line up in sequence. The decluttering of awareness gradually reveals the expanseless expanse of awareness that has ever been the radiant ground of humanity, a radiance both hidden and manifest in the mystery of God in Christ. Nothing is added to reactive mind to turn it into receptive mind. Quite the opposite. The practice of contemplation proceeds by the gradual removal of layers of clutter so that the radiant ground of light now shines less lumbered and encumbered.

Receptive mind sees and reacts to life in a manner different from reactive mind, but all that characterizes reactive mind remains and can suddenly return to dominate rather than allow, behold, listen, and let be. After sufficient decluttering, and the resulting simplification of our inner sight, receptive mind has room to shine forth, while reactive mind tends to dominate less and less—at least in our better moments.

FOUR

A Brilliance Dimly Lit

Receptive Mind

The Lord himself will fight for you;
you have only to keep still.
—Exodus 14:14

If you form an image of God, you make
an idol of God.
—St. Gregory of Nyssa

. . . a darkness all of light.
—Franz Wright

INTRODUCTION: THE RIB CAGE
OF FAILURE

It is simple enough to lose sight of the liberating nature of
our failings. They often seem to lead us into some parched,
lonely place—a place of dry bones. The problem is not
our inadequacies, much less the freight of the failures we
carry, but the loss of perspective on what we resent most in
ourselves. Light forever shines from within the rib cage of

failure. But reactive mind is too cluttered to realize that this is the nature of divine love: flowing waters of mercy for all who are parched—each of us (Jn 4:14; Jn 7: 38). Nor is reactive mind capable of receiving this simple and simplifying fact: *this rib cage of failure is the sanctuary of divine breath breathing us* (Gen 2:7). As we have heard St. John of the Cross express it: "The soul that is united and transformed in God breathes God in God with the same divine breathing with which God, while in her, breathes her in Himself."[1] One is hard pressed to fathom life more utterly created and cradled in Light.

Divine Love is intimately at home with our faults and failings and indwells what we hide from, just as Adam and Eve hid the beauty of their suddenly shameful nakedness behind the trees of Eden (Gen 3:8–10). With hands softened by caressing the lanolin-rich wool of her universal flock (Jn 10:14), Mercy Herself soothes, softens, and loosens the clenched fists of reactive mind.

We who think God is on the lookout for our every fault and failing, in order to catch us out, prove that our vision is still heavily lumbered (Mt 7:5; Lk 6:42) and hence unaware of God's radiant ground shining within all and through all.

To the extent that the mind is dominated by the clutter of inner noise, we are caught up in endless cycles of envy, rivalry, and violence (Gen 4:8), whether within ourselves, within our families, among nations, or within the twisted minds of those who somehow turn ploughshares back into swords (cf. Is 2:4).

With hearts hardened by perfectionism, self-consuming careerism (Ez 36:26), and the competitive rivalry that masks our own life-pain, reactive mind perceives as *intrusion* what is in fact Divine *intimacy*—the circulation of very loving light.

RECEPTIVE MIND: THE SCENT OF WHAT PRAYER IS

It bears repeating that no extra effort or ingredient turns reactive mind into receptive mind. It is the exact same awareness. Receptive mind is simply less cluttered. It is a brighter manifestation of the fullness of Light itself that is ever the grounding Ground of our being. Again, Meister Eckhart puts it: "God's ground is my ground, my ground is God's ground."[2] Receptive mind differs from reactive mind by virtue of expanding inner stillness and spaciousness, intrinsic to awareness itself, which can now emerge more fully, due to the decluttering process of the practice of contemplation. It is important to emphasize that this luminous vastness, which begins to expand as our practice transitions from reactive mind to receptive mind, is not an extra quantity of vastness that has been added into the mix. Ever flowing, luminous vastness has always been shining like the sun. As Franz Wright so brilliantly puts it,

> And I have heard
> God's silence
> like the sun[3]

It is always present and does not know how to be absent, for the simple reason that there is nowhere for it to go. It only seems to be increasing because the decluttering effects of practice allow the luminous vastness of awareness (not the objects of awareness) to emerge in brighter fullness. More space has been freed up as more mental clutter has been cleared away by habits of consistent practice. We are not in control of this process: practice alone will not bring it about, although without the cooperation of our dedicated, consistent practice, little clutter will be removed. It is easy to gain the impression that our practice pulls this off. More precisely we cooperate with what grace is already trying to clear.

When the sun breaks through clouds it doesn't indicate an increase of sun. The sun has always been fully shining. It is the gradual breaking through of what has always been there. The sun does not know how to do anything other than shine. And so it is with receptive mind. Nothing has been added to reactive mind. It is simply that more mental clutter has been cleared. Less mental clutter means that receptive mind is more fully revealed. Receptive mind itself is not yet fully decluttered but it is far more luminous and free than the dark clouds of the heaped-up mental clutter of highly habituated reactive mind. Certainly clouds will re-gather and disperse again and again, but now we know with greater assurance that the sun shines fully, no matter the presence or absence of cloud, mist, fog, or gloom.

Remember very young children before they discover that playing peekaboo is fun and not a travesty? Our disappearance behind the pillow or sofa sets off an explosion of crying and wailing. The child cannot see us. Therefore we are not there. But soon enough the young child crosses a developmental threshold and learns that our action does not mean painful abandonment but playful hiddenness. We suddenly reappear saying, what could not before have been said with any benefit, "peekaboo!" The child squeals with delight. What had been sudden and threatening loss of our stable presence is now a game. Psychology calls this object-permanence. Theology in its own proper way calls this presence-in-absence. When dark clouds return to cover the sun we now realize with calm assurance that the sun continues to shine as splendidly as ever. The sun can do but one thing: shine.

Put another way, reactive mind differs from receptive mind just as hard, dry soil, full of clay, differs from soft, well-worked soil that is rich in organic material. In each case it is soil, but there is a difference in the quality of the respective soils. If we drop a tennis ball onto hard dry clay, the ball will bounce and roll until it settles. But if we drop the same tennis ball onto soft, well-worked soil, rich in organic matter, the soil immediately receives the ball; no bouncing; no rolling. Hard, dry soil is much in need of water but cannot receive or absorb it easily. If there is a heavy downpour, there will be quite a lot of run-off that can contribute to flash flooding. However, well-worked soil receives rain with little or no run-off or pooling. Its receptivity is not passive. It is a generous receptivity that contributes to the life all round it: plants of every sort, birds who nourish themselves and their families on grubs of every kind, good grubs that eat the bad grubs, who have already eaten microscopic creepy-crawlies, and so it goes. Reactive mind needs what it is given but cannot easily receive it, absorb it, and in turn give to the life around it. Receptive mind receives in such a way that it gives. It does this without trying to, simply because it is its very nature to give.

The expansion of reactive mind into receptive mind has nothing to do with the presence or absence of thoughts. The assumption that a maturing practice somehow gets rid of distracting thoughts and feelings is itself the naïve, ego-protecting presumption of reactive mind: get rid of what we do not like and grasp what we prefer. The practice of contemplation does not attempt to cast aside or clench its teeth around anything. The practice of contemplation has no opinion on the matter. It is too simple to get involved in any of that. Practice simply assists with relentless gentleness the necessary healing and clearing away of a lifetime of (often self-inflicted) pain and transgression that keeps us, as St. Bonaventure is fond of saying, "bent over on ourselves."[4] We are caught as if in a tight crawl space in the attic of a deluded mind, unable to fathom that, as John's Gospel puts it, "In my Father's house there are many mansions" (Jn 14:2).

To describe the expansion of awareness that marks this subtle transition from reactive mind to receptive mind, let us return for a moment to the bee in the phone booth. The constricted space of the phone booth of our heads, in which we can spend most of each day of our lives, makes the presence of the bee far more threatening than the bee has any intention of being. The bee may be exploring the possibility of a new location for the community of the hive or, more likely, the bee is seeking to perform its enormous service to the ecosystem by the pollination of innumerable flowers and then return to the hive with nourishment for the entire colony. The poor bee that mistakenly made its way into the phone booth, attracted perhaps by a left-behind sugary soft drink, is misperceived as an exaggerated threat. In fact the bee, having detected our presence, is desperately looking for a way out of the booth, but we decide that its sole intention is to remain and persecute us. What we are frightened of is frightened of us.

But once we extricate ourselves from the phone booth and stand in wide-open space, we may witness many bees simply doing what bees are meant to do. The very same bee is no longer the threat we thought it was when we thought our identity was the constricted space of reactive mind. We experience the formerly threatening bee in a different manner. The bee of distraction now appears in a more expansive, less constricting space. The difference? Previously we experienced our lives as easily threatened, threats to which we automatically reacted. This knee-jerk reaction is due to the dominance of mental clutter and *not to the actual presence of threat*. Receptive mind perceives the same bee in more expansive inner spaciousness. We don't even have to attend to the bee as it goes about its service to the ecosystem through pollination or to the bee's bringing home nutrition for the life of the hive.

Our thoughts have not gone anywhere, but our relationship with these thoughts has changed from subtle (or not so subtle) perception of threats to a humble and receptive allowing the appearance of the simple truth of things. The poet Kevin Hart expresses his desire to be shown truth:

> That slows the blood
> And has the day peel off its shining skin
> And brings bee angels closer just to smell
> What prayer is[5]

Receptive mind is characterized by a growing sense of inner spaciousness. This inner spaciousness presents itself to the perceptive faculties as *always having been present*. Moreover, this inner spaciousness presents itself in such a way that we cannot honestly doubt it.

The inability to doubt this inner spaciousness differs in quality from our crass inability to doubt the appropriateness of our behavior: how we spoke to our spouse or behaved toward a friend or colleague. The inability to doubt the emergence of inner spaciousness is of a different sort altogether. It is self-authenticating. The expanding spaciousness of receptive mind is intrinsically trustworthy. There is no need to ask ourselves, "Is this trustworthy?" Moreover, this inner spaciousness, perceived as always having been present, is at the same time always new. Nevertheless we do well to present this to someone with more experience than we have, who has a clearer eye to confirm it. For we each will ever have our blind spots. What better reason to form a community of those who seek the obvious?

Receptive mind reveals a changing relationship with thoughts, whether distracting or attracting, as well as a deepening insight into the nature of thoughts in general. When we were the phone booth we thought we *were* our thoughts, an entire hive of thoughts in our heads. But with the emergence of receptive mind, thoughts and feelings gradually yield any claim on identity—so impermanent and shape-shifting are they.

Whatever we once thought identity to be, now begins to register as an increasingly obvious inner spaciousness. Mind you, we still have to pay our taxes, buy groceries, and refrain from explaining all these fabulous spiritual things to the police officer who has pulled us over for speeding. This formless inner vastness nevertheless does reveal itself in the most mundane, tragic, joyful, tedious, boring events of day-to-day life, whatever that happens to look like at any given moment.

Receptive mind does not stand over and against reactive mind, as though it were the next stage we must get to in order to advance so that we can then turn around and look at ourselves advancing—and possibly get ourselves officially certified to lead something spiritual as a result. Our practice eventually pries loose the grip that reactive mind has on a good deal (not all) of life-clutter. Space is cleared; clouds disperse. More of the luminous ground previously covered over by clutter is revealed, for receptive mind has been kissed by the "Sun of Justice arising with healing in its wings" (Mal 4:2). As we shall later realize, this is our *patria*, our native land, the graced abode of light sitting in Light. "God from God, Light from Light," in the words of the Nicene Creed. This happens naturally and self-forgetfully, without any bold attempt to make it happen. Of course, we can always get our grips on more mind-clutter.

WHAT IS PRACTICE LIKE?

For the sake of convenience let us presume our practice involves a prayer-word in unison with the breath, a very ancient Christian practice indeed.[6] If it is some other image-free, contemplative practice that cultivates a still body and a still mind—being where our bodies are—we simply adapt as necessary. For most of us the pages of several calendars will have turned before the nature of our practice really begins to ripen and open up. The passing of seasons does not determine when we are ready to give up being interested in our own progress, or our self-centered expectations of what our progress is supposed to look like, as if progress is supposed to look like something that we will be aware of or recognize. This does not mean, however, that a lot of good has not taken place.

Often, we have more emotional balance and physical well-being. Less energy is required to cope with difficult circumstances, and it is common enough to sense increased vital energy (but not necessarily so).[7] We're capable of listening more deeply to others and to ourselves. Sitting in silence is second nature to us simply because silence is our nature, so we settle into it fairly quickly. Moreover, a living and enlivening sense of solidarity with all beings increasingly characterizes receptive mind. More important still, we learn to trust the tangles of loving Providence, as we set out like Jacob into a land he knew not (Gen 12:11; Acts 7:3;

Heb 11:8–9). For "we walk by faith and not by sight" (2 Cor 5–7). But at some moment, when we spontaneously stopped looking at ourselves as objects of fascination, we cease using the practice of contemplation as a means of controlling any aspect of our progress in contemplation. Each time we sit, it is as though for the very first time and we are too innocent to expect anything at all.

The nineteenth-century Russian monk Theophane the Recluse advises: "Delve deeply into the Jesus Prayer. . . . It will draw you together, giving you a sense of strength in the Lord, and will result in your being with Him constantly whether alone or with other people, when you do house work and when you read or pray."[8] The Jesus Prayer is Theophane's practice. While the Jesus Prayer Tradition is an ancient one (and very commonly practiced today in both Eastern and Western Christianity), this does not mean it must be our practice. The point here is that the advice he gives, "delve deeply," indicates a significant maturation of our practice. Such advice would have made no sense to us when we practiced in reactive mind. Had Theophane's advice been, "Return constantly to the Jesus Prayer," that would have made more sense as we practiced in reactive mind. We know this practice: whenever we notice that our attention has been stolen we gently return our attention to the prayer-word in unison with the breath. And so we return and return and return. Yet at some moment ripe and ready (calendar time has no say in the matter), a depth-dimension, so to speak (what Theophane is suggesting by delving deeply), opens up *from within* our practice itself and receives us as though we were one with it. We cannot conjure this. Our practice, which had seemed to be a mental construct to which we always returned our attention, is now not a construct at all but a vast, open space considerably free of the many conceptual constructs formed by the thinking mind (though there remains some residual mental construct to our practice, which is perfectly normal). In reactive mind we were totally unaware of what is now plain as day. Reactive mind simply does not register this depth-dimension, which has always been present. This newly uncovered depth-dimension remains, however, present in reactive mind as non-clinging *longing*, a longing for the pulsing Truth of life that we think we lack and therefore seek as for something lost. Receptive mind, however, easily registers this depth-dimension within practice itself. And so we release into our practice, "Delve deeply," as Theophane says. "Put out into the deep and lay down your nets for a catch" (Lk 5:4).

When our practice opens up from within, it is common enough to perceive, however faintly, that we are being integrated into some larger mystery. Susan (let us call her) describes this as best she can: "As I sat there, it was as though something very loving was drawing my attention deeper into an alluring darkness that seemed to break my heart open. It was a love both giving and at the same time drawing me ever more deeply into itself. None of this seemed to require my permission. For me this would have been a way to control what was simply happening without my permission. Perhaps at some point I had already agreed. But this came as sheer gift. My usual mistrust of anything that my mind could not control was simply not there. It seemed as though the only way to cooperate was to be taken into something entirely loving and trustworthy. This continued for about two weeks." Susan's description is worth pondering. When she was practicing in reactive mind, the inner clutter would have prevented her from this new awareness. She simply would not have been able to see what she described. Nor, due to her mistrust of anything her mind could not control, would she have been inclined to cooperate at all. She would have perceived the darkness not as alluring, but as a threat. Trust would have been out of the question.

Perhaps for the first time we have a limited sense of what it means *to be silence*, instead of actively seeking or longing for the silence we think we lack and trying to make space for silence in our lives, as if this silence were not already silence but some sort of object to be sought and found. This would make sense to reactive mind, to minds fascinated and dominated by concepts of silence. But for receptive mind the distant echoes of home are not so distant as they once seemed. This perceived distance is the fabrication of mind-clutter.

The sheer generosity of receptive mind continues its expanse, an expanse generous enough to cradle in its arms the joys and burdens of a lifetime. Pain still hurts. Joy still gladdens. Despair still flattens. But we are less demanding that the present moment—whether pain, boredom, or bliss—be other than it happens to be. Especially right now.

As the nature and dynamic of our practice expands from reactive mind to receptive mind, so it changes our *relationship* with distracting thoughts. It is not that somehow we have prayer-worded them into oblivion and can now jubilantly proclaim the distracting thought, "I have no more distracting thoughts!" Trying not to have distracting thoughts is a very old trick of reactive mind. As St. Teresa of Avila has often reminded us: "By trying not to have thoughts, we hopelessly stimulate the imagination."[9]

In receptive mind the very same distracting thoughts continue to come, go, or remain, but now, owing to the decluttering of our mind, inner silence expands. These distracting thoughts no longer appear to be so aggressively in our face. They lose their staying power because our practice of inner vigilance allows us to relax the talons of our grip on them. At one time we were convinced it was the afflictive thoughts that had their grip on us. Why is this so?

Our relationship with distracting thoughts has gradually changed from the frenzy of incessant mental chatter to a far less cluttered receptive mind that allows what is simply to be.

The skills of interior vigilance and the resulting inner stillness of our gaze have made possible this changed relationship with distractions. The bee that was a threat is now God's messenger, feeding on the nectar of silence while its legs grow heavy with pollen.

Our practice is now second nature to us and there is also something distinctly different from how practice seemed in reactive mind. A subtle quality—call it silence, interior spaciousness—that we can "delve deeply into," in Theophane's words, by means of release, introduces self-forgetful abandon into our practice. The anonymous, fourteenth-century English author of *The Cloud of Unknowing* describes well this qualitative difference. At the close of Chapter 7 he encourages the use of what we now call a prayer-word. It is noteworthy that his teaching is directed toward those at the beginning of the practice of contemplation and hence dominated by reactive mind. He advises: "fasten this word to your heart, so that it never parts from it, whatever happens."[10] Obviously it does happen; so we simply return our attention to the word, which wraps and enfolds our intention.[11] The author has us going at thoughts with the weapons of a soldier in battle. The prayer-word is like a "shield" or "spear." We are to use this word "to hammer down every thought beneath the cloud of forgetting; so if any thought forces itself on you to ask what you have, answer it with no more than this one word."[12] The advice not to get caught up in any dialogue with thoughts that arise is well taken, but the author has us going gangbusters at distracting thoughts, with hammer, spear, and shield. This only reinforces their apparent grip on us, as though they had a substantive reality like that of a rock or plank of wood—substantive enough to be hammered down or lanced with a spear, as we protect ourselves from thoughts with the shield of our contemplative practice. Practice such as this indicates reactive mind. On the basis of this we might think that his teaching is undeveloped. On the other hand, he might simply be adapting his teaching to a readership that, in Chapter 7, is just getting a practice established. He knows how a distracting thought "forces itself on you" and reassures us that if we "hold firm" to our practice, we may "be sure that the thought will not stay."[13] As we shall see, his teaching on the practice of contemplation later changes considerably.

WHAT IS EGO LIKE?

What we said of ego in reactive mind bears repeating here. We are not using the term in the way it is used in many clinical or psychotherapeutic settings. A healthy ego needs a certain strength for proper psychological functioning, to maintain balance in the psyche as whole. But here we speak of ego in a nonclinical way.

Due to its tight knot of psychic energy, the ego of reactive mind appears to have lost the foundational characteristics of awareness itself: light, vastness, flow. The ego of receptive mind is not a different ego, but the same ego in the process of being decluttered, unknotted, less bent over on itself. A sort of healing, we might say, by way of integration into something beyond the grasp of reactive ego. A number of spiritual teachings seem to send ego off to the gallows with a solemn decree: "Death to the ego." It all sounds a bit dramatic, like the Queen of Hearts in *Alice in Wonderland* shouting, "Off with their heads!" Taken the wrong way, it sounds suspiciously egoic. Reactive ego thrives on efforts to conjure its own demise. How dramatic and heroic it all is!

The remarkable thing about the transition from reactive ego to receptive ego is its unremarkable quality. This is because it largely takes place out of our sight. With less mental clutter, receptive ego doesn't snag awareness as it once did. Because the ego of receptive mind does not get in the way of awareness as it did when it was the ego of reactive mind, it can now begin to flow as it is meant to flow in any process of expanding awareness. Many speak of ego as "dying"; we might say instead that it is more deeply immersed in the expansive flow of awareness itself. Here it does not block the flow of psychic energy, but can now contribute to the overall balance of the psyche.

Jesus says, "I come to bring life, life in abundance" (Jn 10:10). Even reactive ego seeks life, but it is hard pressed to receive life in abundance *by itself*. Reactive ego's tightly drawn knot of pain, fear, clinging, and rejection does not know how to receive—it always feels threatened and on the defensive. It resists the tremendously relieving process of being softened and loosened into receptive ego. The egoic fists of reactive mind still grasp but now do so now with far fewer spasms. Its palms have been softened by love's lanolin and can now open up and receive "life in abundance."

The "Sun of Justice" (Mal 4:2) melts egoic ice into water, reactive ego into receptive ego, which now flows into a stream. In turn the stream flows into creeks, rivulets, each with ever more abundant communities of ecosystems, and then into the mighty river that seeks but one thing: *ocean*. This is how reactive ego undergoes a conversion and is integrated into the ego of receptive mind: all this by means of flow into more abundant life.

We have spoken so much of reactive ego in this section on receptive ego because the antics of reactive ego are more clearly seen from the (still limited) vision of receptive mind. The ego of receptive mind is comfortable in silence, not driven by fear and threat, more compassionate, service-oriented, and reliably committed to balancing the psyche as a whole, which leads to still fuller integration into the swelling waters of life that flow toward the open sea.

Nevertheless! Reactive ego has a way of breaking free of all this and knotting itself again into something frightened, freighted, taught, and hard. Despite reactive ego's seeming conversion to taking on the characteristics of flow, it can indeed regress: "This is *mine!* It's *all* mine. You're all about *me.* Why can't you just *see?*" Somehow it will all be OK.

CONTEMPLATIVE SKILLS

In the chapter on reactive mind we saw that certain skills (again, not techniques) began to develop as the fruit of a committed practice of contemplation. Their development, along with the appearance and growth of new skills, continues to be cultivated in the less cluttered and therefore more expansive fields of receptive mind. In this section we shall focus on some of these skills that come to the fore in receptive mind.

We do well to remember that receptive mind does not involve an addition of something extra to reactive mind. The removal of clutter from the floor reveals more open floor space that was always present. Just as sunlight burning through fog does not imply an increase in the sun's brightness but rather the dispersal of fog, so receptive mind involves no new addition, simply more clearing away of a lifetime's mental fog. Three skills merit especial attention: (1) subtler skills of awareness; (2) the skillful use of thoughts be they afflictive or noble; (3) sitting without sitting.

Subtler Skills of Awareness: From Awareness to Aware-ing

With the decluttering and calming of reactive mind, we might have perceived interiorly a flowing current of release and relief and, just round the corner, a sort of healing realization. This realization carries over into receptive mind. For perhaps the first time in our lives we are aware of the enormous extent to which we have (perhaps for many decades) taken these things to be ourselves: a parade of ballooning thoughts, spasms of inner chatter, scratching our compulsion to blame, victimizing designs we have on ourselves, others, and even on life itself—all the cunning that mental clutter accrues. The liberating insight is: that in us which *sees* clutter is free of all clutter. Otherwise we could not see the clutter that we once thought we were. We begin a slow (sometimes not so slow) realization that what we had once taken to be ourselves has no power to stake the claim on our identity that it once did. This does not lead to any confusion regarding who we are, but to the abiding clarity of inner freedom. We realize more clearly than before that we are the mountain and not the weather that appears around the mountain. Whether storms or sunshine, the mountain accepts without judgment whatever weather is weathering. In fact the mountain has no opinion on what weather is weathering. Such is the non-clinging of the mountain's ancient wisdom.

We ourselves do not clear clutter. Our attempts to do so simply increase it. The decluttering of the mind follows quite naturally from the momentum generated by the self-forgetful release into our practice. The bright clarity of awareness itself now begins to reveal itself to us as always having been present. Only gradually does it dawn on us, even here in receptive mind, just how vast is the inner silence that is awareness. When we first become aware, such silence appears to the thinking mind as having a beginning. But to the yet higher (or deeper) mind the silence of awareness has forever been aware-ing, graciously *eternal* in the groundless ground of being. For some the light of awareness is a gradual dawning in deeply receptive mind. For others it might be a thunderbolt of breakthrough. Neither is privileged over the other. Nor is one to be actively sought over the other (this would only add more clutter). Whether gradual or sudden, each is the revelation of the unadorned, naked simplicity of what is. It is this naked simplicity—naked of concepts, claims, and conniving—that is important and not the manner of its advent.

The skill developed in receptive mind is this: less hindered by clutter, we are able to shift our attention from what we are aware *of* to the *aware-ing itself*. When this occurs, the mind is immediately drawn to silence. As we have said, that in us which clearly *sees* the clutter is both clutter-free and *free of the stories we tell ourselves about the clutter*. Otherwise we could not be aware of it.

In reactive mind, whenever our attention was stolen by a distraction, our attention immediately clung to the distraction. The clinging mind immediately produced a story in our heads about what or whom we are angry *at*, envious *of*, ashamed *of*, puffed-up *about*, greedy *for*, envious *of*. But now, in receptive mind, characterized by a liberating release into our practice and hence cleared of so much mental clutter, all the prepositions fall away. We easily shift our attention from what we are aware *of*—anger, joy, fear, pain, shame, happiness, peaceful recollection, pride, despair, what have you—to the *awareness itself*, the very aware-ing, before the clinging mind whisks up a frothy story *of* anger, joy fear, pain, happiness, recollection, pride, despair. When the "of" falls away there is quite simply no one there to launch a story to tell, no video to play, no one there to comment, chatter, or cling. There is simple joy, fear, pain, happiness, peace, pride, despair that is naked of all narrative. There is no isolated, separate self to whip up all these stories in our heads.

In reactive mind this would have been impossible to perceive: for the thoughts and the frothed-up stories we tell ourselves about them (as well as to anyone else who will listen) seem to be one and the same. But in receptive mind, practice is clearing ever more mental clutter from the floor space of our minds, revealing more clearly the radiant ground of all. This radiant ground is already the pure vastness of an expanseless expanse. But remaining clutter prevents us from realizing this, or that our identity is constantly bathed in this light. We may not realize the fullness of the sun's splendor because of the density of cloud cover. Yet the sun shines in its fullness just the same. Similarly the vast and radiant core of all being is already unspeakably vast and radiant despite the abundance of noise and clutter in our heads. This will continue to dawn in luminous mind, as we shall see.

Let us return to the metaphor of the bicycle wheel. It is full of spokes. The spokes are connected to both rim and hub. In reactive mind, our attention is fixed on the rim of the wheel where the spokes are most distant from one another. In receptive mind we can shift our attention from the rim of awareness to the hub of the aware-ing itself—free of any commentary, including the pasted-up, isolated, noise-ridden, independent self. When we do this, the thinking, calculating, screeching, self-loathing, seeking-for-an-object, reactive mind is immediately drawn to silence; that is, until we try to look at it and try to turn awareness into an object. Then we find ourselves yet again strutting and parading on the parapets of delusion, "I am aware of awareness." This is not what this skill is about. Awareness is not an object. Simple, receptive mind is spacious enough to allow the simple shift from what *we are aware of* to the intimate, groundless ground of *aware-ing itself.*

The Skillful Use of Thoughts Whether Afflictive or Noble

If we neither push away nor cling to thoughts and feelings, be they afflictive, run-of-the-mill, or edifying thoughts of God, what are we supposed to do with them? Nothing. We let them be there if they happen to be there. In reactive mind we were more or less always bouncing off the story we told ourselves about them—about everyone and everything. Bouncing off this thought or ricocheting off that thought had the effect of generating story upon story to such an extent that we derived a sense of identity from our tightly-wound world of thoughts. Or, to complicate matters further, we derived a sense of identity based on what we thought others must be thinking of us. We bounced off them only because they appeared at the time to have sufficient permanence or substance to bounce off of. Next thing we know, we've been elected to public office.

Variations of this sort of thing may continue in receptive mind, but after sufficient decluttering we begin to see the nature of thoughts: they are empty. They simply do not possess the permanence required to host our parasitic narratives of a separate self. Receptive mind receives this wisdom: what once appeared permanent and durable is in fact completely see-through, utterly transparent to *very loving Light*. Now we are poised to practice what the author of *The Cloud of Unknowing* reserved to this season of practice: looking over the shoulders of distraction into something else. This would not have been possible for the less seasoned audience whom the author of *The Cloud* instructed in Chapter 7. Addressing a considerably more seasoned audience in Chapter 32, he teaches a far more skillful use of thoughts: "Do your best to pretend not to know that [thoughts] are pressing so hard upon you . . . and try to look over their shoulders, as it were, searching for something else—and that something is God, enclosed in a cloud of unknowing."[14] This requires a considerably more skillful use of thoughts. Thoughts that had previously pummeled us we can now use to steady our gaze into what Meister Eckhart calls "breadth without breadth, expanseless expanse,"[15] "God, enclosed in a cloud of unknowing." What had previously fragmented us now helps steady us. This gaze is the eye of silence cleared of much clutter.

As obvious as this may seem regarding afflictive thoughts it is also true of noble and pious thoughts about God. The fourth-century monk Evagrius addresses this in his *Chapters on Prayer*. When we are in deep prayer, "the demons no longer come upon [us] from the left side but from the right. That is to say, they suggest the semblance of God to [us] in the form of some image that is flattering to the senses, in the hope of leading [us] to think [we have] attained the aim of prayer."[16] We think we have attained union with God because we have had a vision of God! How lucky! We have dressed God in images and concepts, making it seem that God is a particular thing alongside everything else in the universe. The problem is that we have attempted to pin God down with concepts. God is more intimately present than concepts can fathom. This is why the practice of contemplation does not attend to concepts. God is not a concept. Hence, Evagrius's familiar description of prayer as the "letting go of concepts."[17] His more famous colleague, the fourth-century bishop and theologian St. Gregory of Nyssa, states it more firmly: "If you form a concept of God, you make an idol of God."[18]

Sitting Without Sitting

Times of the day reserved exclusively for sitting in silent prayer remain fixtures in our lives for the rest of our days. Now the subtle buffer of thoughts that in reactive mind separated us from our practice is revealed in receptive mind to have been an illusion conjured by our own inner noise, practice has become a *way of being*. Even in our dedication to times of formal practice, it is not as though we are sitting here practicing a practice. There is no separation between our practice and us. This is because the "between," which implies a distance between a subject and separate object, falls away (or has very nearly fallen away). This is immensely freeing; for it allows the leaven of practice to rise and expand. As a result of this expansion our entire life, life as it happens to be at any given moment, is simplified. Indeed life does have an utterly reliable way of being just how it happens to be at any given moment. Only the ever-calculating, hyperactive reactive mind attempts to throw a cloak of denial over the simple suchness of right now.

Practice is both simple and simplifying. By sheer grace something precious opens up from within our practice itself. All of the joys and difficulties of life, be they cause for rejoicing, utterly mundane, or completely derailing are the prayer bench, the chair, the bed that illness has turned into a home, the prayer cushion themselves.

We are liberated from our impatience with the line of people before us at the grocery store. This is our prayer cushion. People doing the most curious things in traffic need not provoke ire, but can be met with calm abiding in the present moment in which all this potentially dangerous nonsense is occurring.

We are accustomed to practicing with thoughts that arise from within as we sit in silence. But because practice itself is inherently self-effacing, receptive, and generous, external situations that provoke impatience, fear, embarrassment are included in the wide embrace of practice itself. We are this practice whenever, wherever, and with whomever we are. This is what the phrase "sitting without sitting" refers to. Life itself has become a prayer bench, an invitation to practice, simply because we are.

This is especially good news. For whenever the reasoning mind, which is clean, clear, and remarkably silent no matter the complexity of the intellectual task, is not doing what it is created to do (reason, invent, create, administrate, explore possibilities, etc.) it is usually up to no good. The invitation is to donate ourselves to practice outside of official times. Doing the washing, the ironing, folding the laundry, vacuuming, setting the table, walking from the car to work, grocery shopping, standing in line to pay for the groceries are each gracious invitations to practice just by being. There are so many times throughout the day when our minds are not absorbed in reason's God-given purpose. Instead of giving ourselves the opportunity to blend and shake a reactive cocktail of anxious worry, frothy with commentary on how everybody else (it's always the other guy somehow) ought to behave, we donate our intention and attention to practice. This is a really obvious thing to do; in receptive mind there is a subtle (sometimes not so subtle) deeply alluring quality to practice when, radically decluttered of self-consciousness practice, it has become a simplifying way of being—despite the fact that on more surface levels we may need to wipe away the drool of boredom. (How things happen to feel to us does not have the final word on the deeper truths of hidden things.) We have received a generous invitation to donate ourselves to "sitting without sitting," for the sake of an ever fuller expansion of inner freedom in all aspects of our lives, whenever the thinking mind is not needed. In due course, "sitting without sitting" establishes certain conduits of very loving light that render us vulnerable enough to see.

SPECIAL CHALLENGES

Trying Too Hard

Regularity is the essence of a contemplative practice that matures in response to the enlivening grace within every breath breathed. The maturation of our practice bears fruit in the self-forgetful beholding of what cannot be beheld; there is no object to behold somewhere over there. Nor, as we shall see, is there any separate self to do the beholding. Such are the borders of the boundless. This is quite simply the normal unfurling of the fronds of God in each of us as the Life of our lives. Yet it is impossible to chart, measure, or predict, try as we may, simply because the coordinates of vastness find no foothold.

As committed and consistent as our practice rightly is— our cooperation with grace is essential—there remains the risk of sometimes trying too hard, with the result that we start tripping over ourselves. This is fairly common and easily occurs both in reactive mind and in receptive mind. If we are graced with the ability to laugh at ourselves, this can be rather amusing—the tediously pious don't find any of this the least bit funny.

It is easy to recognize when we are trying too hard. A sense of frustration or inner tension builds up, and suddenly we are pounding our heads against our practice. Or, suddenly bewitched into thinking (yet again) that we control the subtleties of practice, we are bound and determined to pound our practice into oblivion so that we finally convince ourselves that we are *there*! "Good God, I'm spiritual but not religious!" There is no "*there*" to get to by means of our efforts to acquire. Nevertheless, the effortless effort of dedicated practice remains essential.

When we are tripping over ourselves, our breath is out of sync and out of sorts. Short, shallow breathing and inner tension are among the typical signs of this. Sometimes our breath that had been slow and abdominal has now shifted up into the solar plexus or, more distractingly, into the upper quadrants of the lungs. This can bring us to the point of hyperventilating. If this happens, forget about everything you have ever heard about the practice of contemplation. Just stop. Try yawning. Get up and leave the room—anything to get your brain out of your practice. The thinking mind is trying too hard and has become entangled in our practice in an effort to produce an outcome. So we need to get out of our heads and back into our practice by any means at hand: recite the times tables; name the US state capitals beginning with Maine; name the home counties surrounding London; name the birthdays of all the kids and grandkids. The point is that when we are tripping over ourselves we need to distract ourselves from ourselves.

When we have sufficiently tripped over our practice we finally begin to see the cause of it all: we throttle our practice because we think we are actually in charge of our own spiritual growth (whatever that is supposed to look like); we are in charge of the beautiful transformation of ourselves into egoless contemplatives. God, we're gorgeous! The inner tension and frustration created by trying too hard is grace's way of pulling the rug out from under us. We cannot master Silence. Any attempt to do so, no matter how naïve, will backfire. Simplicity is never as tame as we think.

Observing Our Own Progress

The corporate world of the marketplace wants to shape simple awareness into the only thing that counts: constant, measurable progress, in this case spiritual growth, with increasing progress and profit year upon year—that is to say, retreat after retreat. We have paid good money to a retreat house and spiritual director and should therefore see measureable results, "outcomes assessments," which we expect to increase steadily and measurably if we have put in the necessary time and effort. Obviously we get to decide what constitutes "necessary time and effort." This cuts against the grain of contemplative practice by getting us to focus on ourselves, on how "my practice" is coming along.

Focusing on ourselves leads to comparing ourselves with others. This in turn leads to rivalry: "I'll beat you to the finish line of enlightenment." When we presume that our progress in the spiritual life is something we can readily observe or fully understand, we have purchased a lie.

The spirituality marketplace offers certificates in all manner of things, spiritual teachers who have websites about themselves, complete with details of how to friend them on Facebook or follow them on Twitter. It is a far cry from the simplicity observed by the sixteenth-century German poet Angelus Silesius: "The rose blooms without why; it blooms because it blooms."[19] Whether in leaf, bud, or blossom a rose takes no notice of itself. It does not ask itself, "Well now. Shall I bloom today or just take a personal day and bloom tomorrow?" In reactive mind we clearly sit for a "why." Why sit? To acquire something we need and are convinced we do not have, but in fact already are—loving union with God. It is precisely this communion that evokes our beseeching in the first place. Again as St. Augustine puts it, "You cannot love what you do not know."[20] Why don't we long for plaid-flavored ice cream? We don't long for it because it does not exist. Humans do not typically desire what does not exist. We may very well long for chocolate-flavored ice cream. It does exist. We only desire it if we have previously tasted it. And so it is for God. Because in some deep way we know (commune with) "the luminous darkness," as St. Gregory of Nyssa names it,[21] the mystery we call God, we can desire the very God who from all eternity seeks and knows us, thus causing us to seek in return. To seek the Living One is a response to having been found (created) by God.

The maturing contemplative is too poor to be concerned with spiritual progress. If there is a measure of spiritual progress, it will be found in the rib cage of failure: in our debilitating faults, our defeats, our wounds, our solidarity with those who are marginalized from every circle of meaning they belong to. This seems to be the way Divine Love works, to seek out and indwell where we hurt most. This is the obscure realization of receptive mind.

The practice of contemplation simplifies us in such a way that there is nobody there to be concerned about something as pretentious as an observable result or outcomes assessments. There are no such results on the contemplative path. We speak of fruits. "By their fruits you shall know them" (Mt 7:16; 20). Fruit suggests something far more organic, dynamic, and nourishing than mere "results." Fruit bears within it seeds of new life and provides nourishment to others. The fruit of practice is compassion, born of the fragrant wound of solidarity with all that is. It has nothing to do with outcomes assessments. We cannot behold if we are trying to assess.

Let us return, as we have done many times, to St. Paul and what his wounds reveal to him: Three times he asks the Lord to remove what he calls "this thorn in the flesh"

(2 Cor 12:7–8). St. Paul does not ask a mere three times that his affliction be removed. "Three times" is a Hebrew way of saying that St. Paul is forever pleading with God to remove this affliction. God's answer is simple: "No. I am sufficient. You keep these afflictions and be content with me alone." Ultimately Paul finds incarnate in what he loathes most about himself the very Presence he seeks most. "Now I boast in my weakness" (2 Cor 12:19).

How we inhabit our wounds before they have a chance to scar over with fear, resentment, or life-pain, and what we learn from these wounds is beyond the metrics of progress. Yet stillness, insight, and compassion continue to thrive, throb, and swell with Life.

When it comes to the uselessness of our preoccupation with our own spiritual progress, Christian Bobin cautions wisely. In "Mozart and the Rain" he writes: "My God, protect us from perfection, deliver us from any such desire."[22] In "World of Distance" he says, "Holiness is so far from perfection as to be its polar opposite. Perfection is the spoilt little sister of death."[23] The problem is not progress but our attempts to assess it.

Trying to Recreate Experience

When we have some of those high-cholesterol periods of silent prayer, we watch with humble gratitude our lovely, clutter-free prayer. Such periods may even last a few days. However, like all grace, prayer usually works out of sight, and how it happens to feel is not the point. How prayer registers in the feelings is impermanent. It is one of a number of patterns of weather appearing and disappearing in the valley over which Mt. Zion presides. We are the mountain, not the weather. We may remember to remind ourselves of this, but in fact we do not want to hear it. Due to deeply ingrained resistance to the God we seek, we are more interested in trying to recreate a positive experience than in practice no matter our interior weather: torrents of boredom, sand storms of frustrating dryness, sunshine that we welcome, sunshine that beats us down without relent, low-hanging clouds of mood that last and last and last. We have various strategies of wasting time. We might start talking to ourselves: "I had just showered before a period of silent prayer. It left me feeling refreshed and energized. So, I'd better shower first from now on." "I had gulped a cup of coffee which made me more alert. So I'll do that regularly as soon as I get up. Or was it black tea? It might have been green tea. Organic?" "I think I used a different pillow to support my back against the chair. Better posture means better prayer." There is nothing wrong with these things in themselves. There are things we can do to dispose ourselves toward practice. But it stops there. When we use basic things as bait to capture what we have somehow decided prayer is supposed to look and feel like at any given moment, we ourselves have taken the bait and are hooked by the illusion that we are in control of our prayer lives.

Judging Our Practice

The tendency to judge our practice continues in receptive mind. This is based on a rather arrogant presumption: somehow we know how our practice should be. Somehow we know what a dedicated, long-cultivated practice of contemplation is supposed to look like and feel like. We presume that an enlightening contemplative breakthrough must mean that our life-issues, our character flaws, will magically disappear. The enlightened person still feels sick after another round of chemotherapy. The enlightened person still has life-issues. Gets grumpy. Occasionally barks at people on television. Enlightenment does not change this. This is the point of view of the cosmetic contemplative, not that of the enlightened contemplative who is too poor to have anything to defend. Yet we do this nonetheless. When the mystery we call God looks within us and through us, God sees only Himself (how ego-deflating). Yet when we look within ourselves we see someone seeking enlightenment despite the fact that the God we think we seek is already looking out of our eyes; has known us since before we were born (Jer 1:5). What enlightenment does without our asking it to, like the rose that blooms without a why, is engender, sustain, and invite us into a long process of integration of all our issues, faults and failings into our essential, enlightened being. The fruit of this integration is not the sanitization of our faults and transgressions but manifestations of Divine Light through what we may judge to be inappropriate given how long we have practiced and how many retreats we have been on.

Feeling on the Periphery of Things

It is common for contemplatives to feel we are on the periphery of things, without realizing that this is often how life at *the very core of things* registers in our feelings. Until the fullness of this paradox is established (not resolved through logic) in receptive mind, we will likely perceive tensions and conflicts where there are none. A common example of this is the perception of a tension or conflict between the active life, somewhere over here, and the contemplative life, somewhere over there. The more cluttered our heads the more convincing the conflict. The more decluttered our heads, the more expansively inclusive the inner silence and the deeper the realization that there is no such thing as "a between." The sun and its rays are of a piece. There is no between involved. The ocean and its waves are of a piece. A tree and its branches are of a piece. Any distinction we might make has no final claim on the truth of things because our minds are too cluttered to realize that *God is also the distinction.*[24] Some of our pet dualisms, such as that between a true self and a false self (the Lord help us), the dual and the non-dual, the contemplative and the active, the monastic and the . . . goodness knows what, are seriously unfounded and ungrounded in the silent ground of each of us.

This can be painful. We are constantly facing culturally (often religiously) sanctioned forces of exclusion that attempt to counter the intrinsic inclusion of all beings. We often feel quite the misfit, which can easily spill over into the reactive woe-is-me contemplative misanthrope. This is not an easy place to be. But until we have made our peace with this and are content to be the cruciform witness to the living waters, we resist feeling intimately at home in the tangles of loving Providence. The perception of being both on the edge and at the very Center becomes a place of intercessory solidarity. We have often heard St. John of the Cross remind us, "The soul's center is God."[25] God is one with all. Hence, with God as our center, we are one with all. At times this simple truth washes onto the shores of perception. It is only half-glimpsed, but in such a way that leaves us deeply convinced of our place in the spiritual balance of things.

FIVE

An Ocean of Light

Luminous Mind

In you is the fountain of life.
In your light we see light itself.
          —Psalm 36:10

What God is by nature we
become by grace.
          —St. Athanasius

Dunno. . . . I like forget about everything.
I sort of disappear. I sort of disappear.
          —Billy Elliot

INTRODUCTION: AN ARC OF BEAUTY

"Can I ask you just one last question, Billy?" Often enough the spontaneous final question, that "one last question," elicits the type of truth-telling that leaves the questioner taken aback.

Those who have seen the award-winning film *Billy Elliot* will remember this scene. Billy is as surprised as anyone to have received an invitation to audition for a scholarship to one of the world's most prestigious schools for classical ballet, London's Royal Ballet School. For a host of reasons, Billy is a long shot as a candidate and his audition before the august review panel is an unqualified disaster. Billy can't dance in such an intimidating situation. He is too self-conscious. Billy's father is up and out the door and on his way back to the "Thatcher" coal miners' strike in the north of England. Billy, gathering up his things, is not far behind him. But just then there comes a spontaneous question from one of the panel. Perhaps she intuits something in Billy and tries to think of a question that might draw him out: "Can I ask you just one more question, Billy? What does it feel like when you're dancing?" Billy turns around, takes a few seconds to gather his thoughts, and comes out with a hopeless: "Dunno." But he continues, haltingly, "It sort of feels good. It's sort of stiff and that. But once I get going, I like forget everything and I sort of disappear. I sort of disappear." With this answer he captures the attention of the panel. Billy returns to County Durham in the north of England. After an anxious time of waiting, the letter from the Royal Ballet School finally arrives. Billy is accepted.

That final question at the end of the audition allowed him to show that he had already discovered the inner skill of abandon to the deeply freeing demands of the discipline of dance.

Billy's words reach deeply into the Christian contemplative tradition of unknowing as a higher (or simpler) way of knowing. "Dunno. . . . I sort of disappear." Billy was able to give voice to what cannot be voiced. This self-forgetful unknowing has for nearly two millennia attempted to speak of an intimacy with God that runs deeper than our words and concepts can reach. From the earliest centuries of Christianity there have been any number of names for the intimacy of this unknowing: the fire of the mind, the crest of the wave of the mind, the eye of the heart, the eye of the mind, the high point of the soul, and many others. They attempt to name the fullness of human knowing, natural to each and all. Billy discovered this fullness entirely on his own, without seeking it, so natural it is, by the grace of God, to the full-flowering of the human. While Billy reminds us that this happens routinely as a child plays or dances, it matures in the living of life. Billy said, "I sort of disappear." Of course, Billy did not disappear. He became so one with dance that he forgot himself in it. There is powerful witness to this in the closing scene of the film. Billy, now an adult, is dancing the leading role in Matthew Bourne's version of *Swan Lake*. The muscled grace of his entrance on stage reveals to all there present an arresting arc of Beauty. We see Billy's father, a most unlikely ballet-goer, gasp as he too is drawn in to his son's soaring arc.

LUMINOUS MIND

How does luminous mind differ from reactive mind and receptive mind? First and foremost there is no real difference. Mind cannot be divided up into separate parts. However, to reactive mind, and to a certain extent to receptive mind, this seems to be precisely the case. We take as real what is in fact a mirage. It promises to slake our thirst but leaves the throat ever more parched the more we try to drink. This mirage convinces us that simple awareness can indeed be divided up into clearly defined stages, according to invented metrics of measurable spiritual progress. Accompanying the metrics of spiritual progress is the tendency to remain focused on ourselves: "Where can I find myself on the spiritual path?" Often we place ourselves rather high up there, to avoid the liberating struggles and failures, the crushed grapes of our lives.

The simplicity of God is too intimately present for the thinking mind, whether reactive or receptive, to fathom. Nothing has been acquired or added to receptive mind so that we now have something new, which we call luminous mind. Luminous mind is and has ever been the very ground of all, whether reactive mind or receptive mind, an expansive field of bright and boundless clarity that can break through the most cluttered of minds, without any effort on our part.

Imagine a room so heaped with clutter—old magazines, newspapers, invoices, notices of foreclosure, unopened and unposted birthday cards, unfiled tax returns, clothing that no longer fits—that we cannot even see the floor. Mental clutter provides us something to cling to. The practice of contemplation initiates the process of decluttering the mind by means of inner silencing. We ourselves do not make any of this happen. The process is typically painful, especially when it involves the decluttering (purification or liberation) of what used to be called "our higher nature": pride, envy, greed, vainglory, concern with what others think of us—our reputation. These are more painful, because they are more spiritual. The best first response is simply to meet them as Mt. Zion meets the changing patterns of weather—with calm acceptance, gentle indifference, and without commentary. Decluttering will continue to the extent that we do not try to make it happen but instead simply stay out of the way by dedication to our practice and learning how to live gently and silently out of that practice.

Over many seasons of practice, layers of clutter are removed by the liberating dynamism of stillness itself. What is revealed is a vast, dimensionless floor space cleared of clutter, a space that we have perhaps never before seen. This clear floor space is and has always been the radiant ground of all: luminous mind, full and flowering, always present, pure, and simple.

In his Letter to the Romans, St. Paul says, "Do not conform to the pattern of this world, but be transformed by the renewing of your mind" (Rom 12: 2). Seen in the light of the practice of contemplation, renewal of the mind is the manifestation of luminous mind, an ocean of light. When luminous mind swells with such ripeness that it breaks open, there emerges from it the very flower of awareness itself. The flower of awareness "perceives" only the grounding union of all creation in such a way that the particularity of every form of life—all creation—is distinct to the extent that we are all one in the breathing depths of God. Only inner silence resolves these riddles. Their resolution is silence. Cupped in the petals of the flower of awareness is emptiness, in which we live in freedom in the midst of our life circumstances, be they delightful, dull, laden with the burden of getting through the day—in quiet contentment with our circumstances as they happen to be, not the way we hope (deceptively) the practice of contemplation will shape them to be.

VERY LOVING LIGHT

Austin, let us call him, aged six, thought swimming lessons were a great waste of time. There was nothing he could do to prevent his mother from signing him up for a course of swimming lessons. But Austin reasoned that nothing required him to allow the swimming instructor to locate him in the pool.

Austin already swam like a fish. As soon as he saw the swimming instructor approach for the half-hour lesson,

Austin held his breath underwater right beneath the swimming instructor. When Austin finally came up for air, he saw the instructor peering down at him, and immediately torpedoed 25 yards from that side of the pool to the next. He remained there underwater for as long as he could. He reasoned that if he could not see the instructor, the instructor could not see him. When Austin came up for air again, there was the swimming instructor. At the sight of him, Austin swam 50 yards to another side of the very large pool. Having arrived at that end of the pool, Austin took a deep breath and swam underwater for nearly another 50 yards, surfacing underneath the giant slide, which offered a partially shielded view of the entire pool area. With eyes and nose just above water, Austin surveyed the area like a periscope. The swimming instructor was nowhere to be seen. Austin was slightly alarmed; the predator might be lurking in some corner, waiting for the right moment to pounce and strong-arm him into a swimming lesson. Austin then looked toward the pool office on the far left. He spotted the swimming instructor on the telephone and concluded that he was phoning Austin's mother, which of course he was. When Austin got home later that afternoon he found out that the instructor had said: "Mrs. Tankersly, I think we should consider cancelling Austin's swimming lessons this summer. I can't catch him, and he won't let himself be caught. Whether he's swimming underwater or on top, I assure you that Austin is a very strong swimmer and will soon make a valuable addition to our competitive swim team. Right now, I think your money would be better spent on swimming lessons for some of your other children, presuming they allow me to catch them."

We shall return in due course to the giant slide that Austin hid behind, for it occasioned an extraordinary awakening within the child that would deeply affect him for the rest of his life. Austin had been well prepared for what happened in this pool of Siloam (Jn 9:6–8) that healed his blindness to the simple fact that we are each already one in God without our having to try to make it so.

Austin's first-grade teacher, Sr. Marie Antoinette, was a tall, gentle Benedictine nun. She was a sort of mystagogue—one who initiates and guides someone into the depth-dimensions of faith to which children are remarkably open. Perhaps it's to do with their imaginative powers, their sense of wonder, their need to play—to say nothing of their sense of fairness.

Time to play is an essential element in the rhythm of a child's school day. For this age, group play is as important as grammar, reading, music, arithmetic, or phonics. Like everything else in the course of a first-grader's day, the two periods of recess begin and end in the exact same way every day.

As soon as Sr. Marie Antoinette announces that it is time for recess, the children line up double-file at the door in the back of the classroom, which opens straight onto the schoolyard. With barely suppressed enthusiasm, the children wait. Sister gives the word and they bolt out the door into the self-abandon of play. This mayhem lasts 35 minutes, and then the children are summoned back to civility (or a first-grader's version of it) by Sr. Marie Antoinette's ringing of the bell. All the children run at full tilt toward the nun, stopping on a dime just short of running into her. They form a perfectly straight line, double-file, and stand there in complete silence (more or less) until Sr. Marie Antoinette makes a gesture of welcome, which starts the children's procession back into the classroom, each returning to his or her own desk.

Austin is not only a strong swimmer, he is also the fastest runner in his class—*by far.* One day he decides he needs to get to Sister before anybody else does, which he easily accomplishes. You see, Austin has a pressing question to ask. "Sister, what are those slats of light breaking through the clouds over there?" She looks west and says, "That is God pouring Himself into someone. God does that all the time. God is very loving light." Austin asks, "You mean God is sunlight?" The nun replies, "Well, yes." He somehow knows that she has revealed some deep mystery about the hidden truths of life. Austin feels such joy that he doesn't know how to contain himself; he flings himself at the nun, wrapping his arms around her. Enfolded in yards of the black wool of the voluminous Benedictine habit, he is momentarily lost from sight from the rest of his classmates. When Austin emerges some moments later from these woolen layers, his young life is somehow different.

A POOL OF LIGHT

Decades later, now in his forties, Austin reflects on this period of his life. "As a boy I spent the summers at a very posh country club, which had a huge cruciform pool. After a morning of grueling tennis lessons and fiercely competitive matches, I spent the afternoon swimming and sunbathing. But until my first-grade nun had told me that bathing in the sun was to receive God pouring Himself into me as loving light, I had no idea that sunbathing was a way of praying without words. It happened all by itself. I simply lay down for as long as I wanted and received God's own light. Prayer was simply a matter of lying still. I was hugely excited to discover that the procedure for this type of prayer was the exact same procedure for darkening my tan. The more bronzed my skin the more tangible the proof that I was in the presence of God.

I remember looking around at the other sunbathers. I thought, 'They must be praying too.' They lay there, completely silent, while their skin received the very same loving light of God that I was receiving. We were each bathing in and tanned by the same Light. At the time, of course, I had none of these concepts and language. I was only six or seven, but this was my first exposure to silent prayer, just being there. The rest took care of itself. Curiously girls admired my tan and they asked if they could apply suntan lotion to my back. I consented to the procedure, but viewed their overture with over-modest suspicion.

I alternated between sunbathing and swimming. When I was in the pool something kept drawing me back to the huge slide (you had to be ten to go down it, so I had just three to go). It was solidly fixed to the concrete foundation of the pool so that it could not suddenly decide to reposition itself at another location in the pool. I would go underwater and at-tach myself to one of the slide's foundations. This allowed me to be still and make no effort to prevent myself from floating backup to the top. I liked seeing how long I could hold my breath underwater. Over 75 seconds!

I knew there were a lot of other people in the pool but I couldn't make them out underwater. One day I stole my big brother's goggles. Now I could see clearly what things looked like from underwater, which people above the water could not see. Not even my first-grade, mystical nun could have pre-pared me for what I saw when I put on my brother's goggles. Time stopped. All the water in the very large pool was shot through with light. Not just slats of light, but the entire pool *was* light. It did not look like this from above water. I could see clearly all the separate people swimming in the pool. Yet I could not say that I was quite watching them. There were only all these people. They were me. We were all one in the illuminating water of God. We were each individual bodies but at the same time we were all one body. Again, at the age of seven, I had none of this language and in many ways I regret that I now do, for language obscures the simplicity of the simple fact.

One of my sisters told my older brother that I had taken his goggles. He took them back. He hid them someplace where even my sister could not find them. Nevertheless, there remained a strong attraction—or better—invitation to return to that very place. I think my mother sensed that something was drawing me to this large swimming pool. With five children to shuttle from here to there, she would always have time to deposit me at the country club to swim for as long as I liked until I phoned her to say I was ready to come home.

I would return to the very same place under the slide, holding on to the slide's foundations to keep me down at the bottom of the pool. I didn't have my brother's goggles anymore, so did not have the same clarity of knowing that the water was filled with light. I did not know how many people were in the pool when I was underwater. But this unknowing posed no challenge to the realization that each particular being was both itself and God. Between the quiet prayer of sunbathing and the stillness at the bottom of the pool, everything seemed to be God somehow. Even though I am now in my forties, these realizations seem as though they happened just yesterday—maybe not quite that long ago."

Far more than we may realize, children have profound, life-orienting realizations of the eternal presence of God and of God's apparent absence as just another form of Divine Presence. Cloudy skies do not mean that there is no sun. Perhaps because children do not have the words or concepts to make sense of any of this, it doesn't occur to them to try.

Austin had no way of knowing that the saints and sages of the Christian tradition speak similarly of how this un-knowing and oneness are of a piece. The tenth-century, Byzantine monk St. Symeon the New Theologian says, "He is then totally within the depths of the Spirit, just as if he had been dropped into a bottomless abyss of illuminated waters."[1] By the grace of stolen goggles, the eye of the heart opened within Austin, enabling him to see that all things are shot through, held, beheld, and revealed as Divine Light. Austin did not encounter objects of his awareness, but instead realized the breaking open of awareness, the flower of aware-ness which perceives no subject/object dichotomy. St. Symeon continues, "When this happens, that person rises ineffably into perfect unknowing, for the person has transcended all knowledge."[2] St. Symeon uses the term "unknowing." Billy Elliot, without St. Symeon's sophistication, put it as well as he could, "Dunno." St. Symeon's "unknowing" is a term that has been and continues to be used to indicate the overflowing of conceptual knowledge. Concepts cannot contain or grasp the depths of what is presented to them, not out of anything lacking on their part, but out of the simplicity of superabundant Presence. This yields a knowing that only the denizens of Silence both "unknow" and yet proclaim with the surest of knowledge. This surety of unknowing is beyond doubt and beyond speech and yet so intimate that concepts genuflect in that special, humble joy that comes to us as arcs of beauty.

In the course of history this "unknowing" traces its scriptural origins at least as far back as Moses on Mount Sinai. The summit of Mount Sinai is covered by a dark cloud, a symbol of God's shepherding presence to the people of Israel. "Moses entered the darkness where God dwelled" (Ex 20:21). The Psalmist likewise reminds us, "God made the darkness his dwelling place" (Ps 18:11). The sliding of centuries bears witness to this through countless contemplatives and whispers in our own ear, telling us to approach the cloud-covered summit of Mount Sinai naked of all concepts.

St. Symeon also expresses this mystery in the language of light. For, as the Psalmist says, "Darkness is not dark to you, and night shines as the day. Darkness and light are but one" (Ps 139:12). St. Symeon writes, "When the mind is simple, or rather stripped of all concepts and completely clothed in the simple light of God and hidden within it, it can find no other object in which it is established to which it can direct the motion of its thought. It remains in the depths of God's light and can see nothing outside. This is what the saying means: God is light (1 Jn 1:5). God is the supreme light, . . . the repose of all contemplation."[3]

St. Symeon expresses something of what Austin experienced as a boy, when his contemplative practices (though he would not have known the term) were sunbathing and staying underwater for as long as he possibly could. What happened to Austin? He forgot himself. In that timeless moment he was unselfed of himself just as was Billy Elliot in his "Dunno." When we are unselfed of self, we realize what has always been true; we are one in the groundless ground of God. This does not mean that everything becomes some sort of blob. Far from it: all particular forms of life are fully what they are created to be and are, therefore, manifestations of God. This is the paradox at the core of luminous mind. Humans are most fully created to the extent that we become God—once again, as St. Athanasius the Great wrote, "What God is by nature we become by grace."[4] St. Athanasius is treacherously orthodox here. What St. Athanasius and St. Symeon, and a cloud of witnesses before and after them, bear witness to raises only suspicions in reactive mind—while still offering reassurance, guidance, and inspiration. However, to the radically decluttered luminous mind, this is how life appears when the flower of awareness has blossomed. The conceptual distinction that Christian theology makes between Creator and creature

remains a crucial teaching for most Christians. But the unitive gaze of the luminous mind does not *perceive* the distinction. Instead of distinction, luminous mind perceives
vastness. The sponge looks within and sees only the ocean
of God. The sponge looks without and sees only the ocean
of God. All that is within the sponge is the ocean of God,
but not all of the ocean of God is within the sponge. Let us
keep ever in mind St. Teresa of Avila's helpful metaphor: we
cannot separate the rain water of divinity from the pond
water of humanity. The distinction is merely conceptual,
which the luminous mind does not perceive (though intel-
lectually may acknowledge). It is the creating nature of the
rain water (God) to pour out and to fill. It is the created nature of pond water to receive and be filled.[5] Luminous mind
is too simple to carry the burden of conceptual distinctions.
Conceptual thinking will always have its right and noble
place in our lives of creativity and invention, but not here in
the further reaches of the ocean of light. Thoughts cannot
fully plumb human depths.

The Byzantine monk understands the young Austin's
pool of light, as do countless others, among them one
of the great theologians and preachers of our own era,
Howard Thurman (1899–1981). Thurman was a leading
civil rights activist who became a mentor to Dr. Martin
Luther King, Jr. Part and parcel of Thurman's social
activism is his deep intimacy with God, recorded both

in his preaching and in his books. We do well to remember that, as with any contemplative—whether famous or run-of-the-mill—the ground of Thurman's
commitment to the transfiguration of church and society emerges from having overcome the illusion of separation from God.

Thurman recalls walking along the beach somewhere
in Florida. All was still. The ocean and the tides were still
even as they moved. He reflects back, "I held my breath
against the night and watched the stars etch their brightness on the face of the darkened canopy of the heavens.
I had the sense that all things, the sand, the sea, the
stars, the night, and I were *one* lung through which all
of life breathed. Not only was I aware of a vast rhythm
enveloping all *but I was also* a part of it and it was a part
of me."[6] This is a vivid example of the luminous, unitive
mind. We recall how St. John of the Cross expresses in
his own way that he too breathed from this *"one"* lung
of which Howard Thurman speaks. He writes, "The
soul that is united and transformed in God breathes
God in God with the same divine breathing with which
God, while in her, breathes her in Himself."[7] There is
but one breath breathing. It all harks back to Genesis 2:7,
"God breathed into the man the breath of life." God is
the Divine Breath breathing; creation the divine breath
breathed.

AN INWARD SEA

Evelyn is driving in morning rush hour traffic on the down-town section of Chicago's famously infamous Dan Ryan Expressway. She is on her way to a soup kitchen where she has volunteered three days a week for over a decade. Driving on the downtown (or even midtown) section of the Dan Ryan Expressway during rush hour (or any time of the day, really) is an experience difficult to describe. It is at once like taking a ride on an amusement park's most stomach-turning roller coaster (there's no stopping till it's all over) and being water-boarded (always coming up for air but with nothing con-vincing to say). One day, while taking a slight bend to the left, Evelyn relates, "I simply disappeared. Of course, I was behind the wheel of the car and was certainly attentive to all the things you have to be aware of on an expressway where countless cars are racing along at 75 mph. I mean, you may have to brake suddenly, then accelerate while at the same time preparing to change lanes, in order to get over to your exit that's coming up in about 45 feet. But in this case there was simply no 'I' pre-sent. There was no one called an 'Evelyn.' There was simply the driving, the changing of lanes, putting on the blinker—all this was immersed in a deep, flowing silence. I was obviously driving the car and was not oblivious to everything around me. Yet, there was simply the helter-skelter moving of 60 or so cars all in this flow of life. I was simply part of this flow, not an addition to it. In the moment I was not aware of myself as an object that could say 'I' am having this really cool experience. That interpretation of things came later. Clearly the CCTV cameras installed along the expressway captured nothing but the normal, hectic traffic of morning rush hour. This is about as well as I can say it. It's far simpler not to have to hang words on things when there are no proper hangers to hang them on. I was certainly not prepared for the continuation of this flowing silence—the peace—flowing within, without, and around. Everything was one flowing silence. At the soup kitchen, the guests were as they always were: many grateful; many more ungrateful, impatient, or picky; others in need of more assistance like diapers, money for electricity, baby food. This soup kitchen couldn't manage everyone's needs. So, we made a lot of referrals to places that could. There was the usual arguing. There were many of the regulars who were usually drunk or high. All of this was one thing, but 'thing' is not the right word. It was not a particular thing. All the things involved in running a soup kitchen day in and day out were at the same time this flowing river. When I was at home this flow of silence was at times very strong. But gradually it became utterly normal and unremarkable. I would be doing the laundry, mopping the kitchen floor, paying bills, attending a parent-teacher conference to learn what one of my sons had done this time. All the same ordinary stuff of ordinary days was immersed in this flowing, joyful silence. I must say again that I am not talking of being aware of some particular thing called, 'flowing silence.' There was simply a flowing peace and joy in which everything was held—but not held by something separate from any of this.

When I was at home this flow of silence was at times very strong. Palpable undulations. But gradually the undulations stopped, and the flowing silence became normal and unremarkable. I could be doing the laundry, mopping the kitchen floor, paying bills, attending parent-teacher conferences to learn what one of my sons had done *this* time. All the ordinary things of ordinary days *were* this flowing silence. I feel I must emphasize that I am not talking about being aware of some 'thing' called 'flowing silence.' It's too normal and simple to need to be called anything at all. Yet there it is: flowing silence in which we are all held. That's the simple truth of it. This lasted about four or five days, and then moved to the background of everything. It remains the background of everything, the inner lining of everything. My entire life made whole in this and increasingly reoriented and centered by this."

What happened to Evelyn during this excavating period of her life? While Evelyn's realization is deeply personal, it is not singular to her. Given how humans are spiritually put together, the grace of Evelyn's realization is part of the process of our becoming fully natural; that is, as God intends us to be from all eternity. Evelyn's awareness has simply expanded from discursive awareness (consciousness characterized by thoughts, be they noble or delusive) to a simpler, non-discursive awareness—consciousness free of conceptual thinking, consciousness relieved of the fatiguing burden of subject/object dualism, dual/non-dual dualism. Yet, paradoxically, these too are included in this gracious flow.

It is completely natural for a bud to open, revealing petals long prepared for praise—yet undetected by our techno-scrutinizing squint. This blossom attracts bees, among other apostolic pollinators, to drink of its nectar, fill their pollen bags before moving on to other blossoms, taking nourishment from them while pollinating *in unknowing* as they carry on from flower to flower. And so it goes until the bees return to their community. Our ecosystem cannot survive without this pollination. Yet the pollinators do not know they are pollinating. Pollination is an apostolate of unknowing. Nor do contemplatives know they are contemplating. Contemplation is an apostolate of the most loving sort of unknowing imaginable and courses, as does very God, "who is above all and through all and in you all" (Eph 4:6), within, through, and throughout the life that all life lives in the life God lives in us. Our own deepest realization that we are not separate from God is part of a vibrant, spiritual ecosystem that has no boundaries. A more traditional name for this hidden, spiritual ecosystem is *Corpus Christi*, the Body of Christ, in Whom we are all one in such a way that there exists no separate "I" trying to have an experience. I am "me" insofar as I am "we."

The flowering of awareness, this breaking open *from within luminous mind itself*, reveals Wisdom's eternal splendor. "Wisdom is radiant and is easily discerned by those who love her" (Wis 6:12). For Evelyn, this, and all that flows from it in her daily life as lived, is the fruit of a deep exposure—the veiled unveiling of the light-filled suchness of the Life trying to live in her.

Evelyn bears witness to this in her own life, but so have countless others, ancient and modern. The fourteenth-century Dominican friar Meister Eckhart provides another helpful way of making sense of Evelyn's "experience" of the oneness of all things in God. Eckhart, one among a cloud of witnesses, likewise knows what Evelyn herself realizes. He writes, "We [Eckhart himself] are well aware of this light. Whenever we turn to God, there is a light that shines and burns in us, guiding us to what we should do and what we should not do, and giving us all kinds of good instruction, of which we had no knowledge or understanding in the past."[8] Evelyn does not speak of receiving guidance and instruction, but she says, "My entire life of love and service is made whole in this and increasingly is being reoriented and centered more deeply in this."

Howard Thurman writes, "In that glorious and transcendent moment, it may easily seem to me that all there is, is God."[9] Thurman establishes an important link and distinction between this "glorious and transcendent moment" and doctrinal expressions concerning God. "I work at preparing my mind, my spirit for the moment when God comes to Himself in me. When it happens, I experience his Presence. When this experience becomes an object of thought and reflection, it is then that my mind creates dogmas, creeds, and doctrines." Thurman continues, "These are the creations of the mind and are therefore always after the fact of the religious experience. But they are always out of date. The religious experience is always current, always fresh. In it I hear His Voice in my own tongue."[10] Notice that in what he calls a religious experience Thurman himself is not the center; the center is God coming to Himself. At these moments "it may easily seem to me that all there is, is God." There is no separate someone having an experience of a separate object called God. This is why our words fail us. For the mystery of God's way of being present to us is too intimate for concepts and words to fully grasp—this mystery "in whom we live and move and have our being" (Acts 17:28).

Elsewhere, Thurman writes, "The source of life is God." But "there is in man an uncreated element," without which we could not become fully human.[11] This is what is behind his phrase, "God comes to Himself in me." Without the divine breath breathing Adam (pre-gendered humanity) into life, Adam would not have become a living being (Gen 2:7).

To return to Eckhart's Sermon 24, the friar preaches not only of the birth of the Word in Bethlehem but of the Word's birth in eternity and in the soul. All three at once: a divine birth for every aspect of human life. Regarding the birth of the Word in the soul, and this includes each and every one of us, "It is the peculiar characteristic of this birth that it always brings forth new light. It constantly introduces a strong light in the soul with light so much that the light gathers in the being and ground of the soul and spills over into the faculties and the outer self. This happened to Paul too when God bathed him in his light" (Acts 9:3).[12] Eckhart continues, "The ground of the soul, however, is touched only by this and the more you are free of yourself, the more you shall find light, truth, and understanding."[13]

This is not just "mindfulness" as we commonly hear the word used in a variety of secular contexts (it has been a gift for so many), but the blossoming, the breaking open of awareness itself (the very *aware-ing*). Just as we see without ever seeing the eye that sees (retina, optic nerve, etc.), so the flower of the mind cannot be seen, for it is the very beholding itself. The inner eye which beholds luminous vastness is itself luminous vastness. It is the fullness of created identity held in the fragrant emptiness of an open blossom, the flower of awareness.

WHAT IS PRACTICE LIKE?

Practice sifts soul. Whether peaceful, boring, silly, painful, grueling, or simply pathetic (the weather of our lives, whether within or without, matters not), the practice of contemplation amounts to becoming so silent before God that the "before" drops away. When the "before" drops away, so do we drop away. We cease to be an object of our own awareness.

THE PRACTICE OF CONTEMPLATION: A RECAPITULATION

Our practice of contemplation has been greatly simplified since this path first opened wide its arms. It simplifies because we ourselves have been simplified and therefore have become more natural. As the mind has become decluttered so practice is less encumbered by the lumber of egoic strategies, such as practicing so that we might acquire something (for example, inner peace), and hold on to it for dear life. The simplicity of our practice is seen in our taking no notice of its simplicity and letting go of any notion of progress. As John Chapman writes in his *Spiritual Letters*, "Progress will mean becoming more and more indifferent as to what state we are in."[14] No doubt this Benedictine monk of the early twentieth century found his scriptural footholds in the teachings of Jesus: "If you cling to your life you will lose it. But if you lose your life for my sake you will find it" (Mt 10:39). We find the same teaching in Matthew 16:25; Luke 9:24; and Mark 8:35. In John's Gospel, Jesus tells Mary Magdalene that she should not even cling to him—*noli me tangere* (Jn 20:17)—"Do not cling to me." Clinging would only get in the way of her deeper, non-clinging receptivity of the Crucified and Risen One as the Life of her life, the Being of her being. Centuries later, St. John of the Cross likewise cautions: "It is seriously wrong to have more regard for God's blessings than for God himself: prayer and non-clinging."[15] The Carmelite friar also says,

> To come to possess all
> desire to possess nothing at all.[16]

Here is a brief review of the different forms that practice can take as our minds become free of the domination of mental clutter:

Reactive Mind. For the reactive mind our daily practice, especially at the beginning, seemed to involve a good deal of bouncing off the sides of the phone booth of our head, bobbing and weaving in fear of that bee that means us no harm but poses a great threat to the isolated ego. Our practice rightly emphasized returning to our practice (often a prayer-word or phrase united with the breath or a simple focus on our breathing—each is ancient Christian contemplative practice). The practice was simple: whenever we became aware that our attention had been stolen by a distraction, we simply returned to our practice without judgment of any kind. The practice of contemplation is always a judgment-free zone. Practice is not concerned with having no thoughts or pushing away thoughts or attempts to "blank the mind," but with a simple return to our practice. We allowed thoughts to be present if they happened to be present, which they undoubtedly were. We simply grew in awareness of when they stole our attention. When the attention either attached to or rejected a thought-feeling, a story or inner commentary concerning ourselves, our life circumstances, how other people ought to behave, ensued. The inner commentary, the inner chatter, the inner video that we watched and replayed again and again and again created such momentum that we derived a sense of identity from this inner noise. We easily reinforced this by looking around and comparing ourselves with others as though they provided a sort of measuring stick by which to assess the value of our derived identity as well as our own progress on the path of contemplation. As a result, we usually found ourselves wanting, when in fact at any given moment our practice is *exactly how it should be.* The inner stories we tell ourselves sustain the illusion that we are separate from God, from one another—some separate "thing" from the mystery of Creator, created, creating, and creative. All these stories are the spawn of the originating story of *blame.* Adam cannot resist blaming God for the predicament Adam now found himself in, "the woman whom *you* put here with me—*she* gave me the fruit from the tree, and so I ate it" (Gen 3:12). In this way, the man turns a life of harmony into a life of blame. "It's not my fault. It's all your fault, God."

In order to face the inner noise of a heavily cluttered mind we learned to investigate the mind directly by cultivating the ancient discipline of vigilance or awareness. What provoked these thoughts? Could we name these afflictive thoughts? Could we see what set them off? Did they team up together or did they work alone? Which of these afflictive thoughts were more of an ordeal for us, and which were more manageable? Under what pressures were we more vulnerable to certain afflictive thoughts?

We began to cultivate a fundamental contemplative skill, getting our attention out of the stories we obsessively told ourselves *about* the afflictive thought or feeling: the story *about* the anger, *about* our greed, *about* our need to blame, *about* our fear, envy, or shame—any thought actually. When we cease to attend to these stories we can let them drop.

Receptive Mind. Expanding inner silence or spaciousness, due to more clearing away of the clutter, characterizes receptive mind. Commonly enough this gives us a sense of inner freedom, which we may never have known before. This inner spaciousness gives us the sense that afflictive thoughts, or any thoughts for that matter, are not as solid or gripping as they once seemed. This comes as a great relief. Whereas before our practice was rightly characterized by a habit of returning and returning to our practice, now there is a subtle shift. It is as if we perceive a certain depth-dimension in practice itself. Somehow returning to our practice becomes a releasing into our practice. It's a natural sort of shift that enables us to forget ourselves in our practice. The best way to hinder this subtle natural shift is *to try to make it happen*.

Releasing into our practice was not an option in reactive awareness; there was simply too much inner clutter that needed to be cleared away before the more spacious receptive awareness emerged. This does not happen quickly, but it can happen suddenly when it does. As we release into our practice, we also release our control over ourselves as contemplative projects to be realized. What, when, or if anything happens is entirely up to God.

Accompanying this change in our practice is a changed relationship with thoughts and a deeper insight into the nature of these thoughts and feelings. This change emerges *from within practice itself* without our strategizing or plotting some scheme to bring it about so that we can possess it and control it.

Only our deeply embedded habits of clinging give these afflictive thoughts (any thoughts) the semblance of permanence. As the twentieth-century Serbian Orthodox monk Thaddeus of Vitovnica writes, "Everything is constantly changing; nothing remains static."[17] Our attempt to find permanence, security, a firm foundation in what is not eternal, is to try to build a house on sand (Mt 7:26) and it sets us up for trouble both within and without. Often enough the thoughts that persecute us lead unwittingly to our persecution of others—the result of our own unacknowledged, deep resistance both to God and to ourselves who remain ever hidden in God. But in receptive awareness those thoughts, which once had the semblance of permanence, have relaxed their stranglehold on us and are now themselves able to contribute to the birth of compassion.

This is what the author of *The Cloud of Unknowing* wants to teach us in his Chapter 32. The afflictive thoughts that reactive mind experienced as a hindrance to progress now adopt a new role of service: they help steady our gaze. For receptive mind, these same thoughts are allowed to be present simply because they are present. This marks a change in our insight into the nature of thoughts. Earlier in *The Cloud* the author teaches beginners on the contemplative path. He suggests the use of our practice (here a prayer-word) as our "shield and spear" and instructs us "to hammer down every kind of thought."[18] At the time this teaching seems salvific; it is tailor-made for practice in reactive mind. It provides us a practical way of dealing with thoughts of any nature (afflictive or pious) during the time of prayer. But for receptive mind, this teaching seems like an incredible amount of work and not especially helpful. In Chapter 7 the teaching is aimed

at beginners in contemplative practice, who tend to meet afflictive thoughts with the reactive armor of shield and spear,
the weaponry of all-out battle. But in Chapter 32 the author's
teaching has changed. He is now speaking to a different audience, more mature and no longer needing to use practice
as weaponry. Weaponry once had its place in our practice,
but no longer. This audience experiences afflictive thoughts
not as a call to battle, but as part of the inclusion in practice of all that is. The author realizes that what we call here
receptive mind is characterized by a changed relationship
with thoughts: from exclusion to inclusion. We are able to see
more deeply, though not yet fully, into the nature of thoughts.
Changing like the weather, they are impermanent and completely transparent. They don't have the solidity or the sense
of permanence they once seemed to have. They can now be
put to better use. He advises us "to look over their shoulders,
as it were, searching for something else—and that something
is God, enclosed in a cloud of unknowing."[19] This would not
have been possible to the reactive mind. But what had been
an obstacle now serves to steady our beholding of the ineffable God in whom thoughts, feelings, stories of all sorts arise
and fall.

Luminous Mind. This summary of what we have seen
of practice in reactive mind and in receptive mind (although no two of us will have the same experience—we
all have different minds), with their increasingly simple

and simplifying dynamics, leads us to consider what practice can look like for the luminous or unitive mind. What about practice in luminous mind? There is not that much to say. It remains important to dedicate time to the practice of contemplation. We show up. We sit. We are. Just sitting, just being. There is no effort involved; this is an effortless effort. We do nothing. In luminous mind our practice is free of any strategy to acquire, possess, and control. We let be what is (pain, gratitude, joy, desperation), without comment or quarrel. This "doing nothing" is quite something. Here our weight on the chair, the prayer bench, or the cushion is our love. Just being. As St. Augustine said, "My weight is my love [*pondus meum amor meus*]."[20] In the context of our practice of just sitting, we can take St. Augustine's words quite literally.

Why has practice become so simple? From the very beginning the final purpose (the first in intention though the last in execution) of contemplative practice has been to render itself useless as a strategy to attain something, in this case enlightenment. Through diligent practice we are relieved of our array of strategies for using contemplative practice to acquire some "thing" that will get us some "where." Practice finds its fullness in poverty. As Madeleine Delbrêl writes in her precious book (as yet not translated into English), *Alcide: A Simple Guide for Simple Christians*, "cling to nothing, not even to poverty."[21]

Practice has become so simple because through practice we ourselves have been simplified. Unselfed of self, there is no separate "I" making an effort to be enlightened. It's a great waste of time. How do we light a candle that is already lit?

In luminous mind we simply sit. *There is no agenda or goal attached*. The seventeenth-century poet Angelus Silesius expresses this with simple beauty in his poem "The Rose" from the *Cherubinic Wanderer*:

> The rose is without why.
> It blooms because it blooms.
> It pays no attention to itself.
> It asks not whether anyone sees it.[22]

WHAT IS EGO LIKE?

A tightly drawn knot or constriction in conditioned mindstream, ego barters in the illusion that it is a kingdom unto itself. It does not perceive what St. Paul knows: that unity and particularity are not separate or rivalrous but of a piece. "As a body is one though it has many parts, and all the parts of the body, though many, are one body, so also in Christ" (1 Cor 12:12).

By grace, practice loosens this ego-knot, with the result that it is slightly less convinced of its isolated independence and less insistent that it be the center of all drama. While neither completely diaphanous nor utterly opaque, in luminous mind ego gets in the way less and less. Fear, anger, threat, or an unexpected tax audit can cause ego to draw tight and constricted again, though never to the same extent as when its rule was supreme. Rarely completely becalmed, it is yet tame. At times its arthritic grip can even softly caress. Only luminous mind softens the palms of ego.

Ego is mostly frightened and parasitic. Its required food is our attention, which it needs to maintain its sense of isolated separation and control. Ego's coinage is illusion; it has crafty ways of purchasing our attention and funding an illusory sense of a separate, contained identity, as well as any number of lifestyles that proceed from it.

Luminous mind realizes that ego is completely insubstantial. We can look straight through it. And what is found if we look for this "we" that is doing the looking straight through ego? Mercifully nothing that can be called a thing. While we possibly began to realize this in receptive mind, it seems now to be undeniably the case. Ego can still somehow or other knot up again into its ball of separate self, creating a convincing sense of separation from God, but it does not last as long. Once the ego-knot has been untied, it never returns to being as tightly drawn as before, and is much more easily untied and seen through and pretty much off to the side.

CONTEMPLATIVE SKILLS

Certain skills emerge and are consolidated in luminous or unitive mind. Most notable among these are (1) we are no longer our own contemplative projects; (2) we develop an abiding sense (not quite a feeling) of our union with all; (3) we finally stop comparing ourselves with others.

A person drawn deeply to silent prayer over decades approached a wise teacher in the ways of prayer. "I want to get prayer down cold," she declared. She clearly meant the techniques of posture, breath, the use of a prayer-word, how much time each day. This person's ego was really into contemplative practice. The teacher responded, "Go home. Come back when you have given up all notions of prayer as a way of getting what you want from prayer." Harrowing words. Indeed, among all of the crucial skills for the practice of contemplation perhaps most important are a richness of desire too poor to seek an object of desire, self-forgetful openness, and blind trust. For "we walk by faith and not by sight" (2 Cor 5:7).

No Longer Objects of Our Own Contemplative Project

We cease to be the goal of our own contemplative project simply because Silence has set us free from being objects of our own awareness. The Psalmist says, "Our soul like a sparrow has escaped from the snare of the fowler. The snare is broken and we are set free. Our help is in the name of the Lord who made heaven and earth" (Ps 127:7–8). The fowler's snare is our complete fascination with how we are faring on the contemplative path.

What causes the flower of awareness to emerge from luminous mind and blossom—break open into mindstream? The teeming vitality of unknowing. Having been unselfed of self, thereby advancing the creative evolution of our kind for the benefit of the entire cosmos, we cease being objects of our own awareness. We are no longer our own contemplative projects, isolated from one another. We saw this in the case of Evelyn: "I simply disappeared." We saw it in the character of Billy Elliot in the eponymous film: "What does it feel like when you're dancing, Billy?" "Dunno. . . . I sort of disappear." Both Evelyn and Billy are empty. Empty of what? Empty of a defining sense of being a separate, isolated self. Each comes to realize that (this goes a bit beyond the script of *Billy Elliot*) what we call a "self" is a simple, unadorned fact: the interconnectedness, the dynamic interdependence of all life. This is the communal nature of being. "In Christ, we who are many are one body and each member belongs to one another" (Rom 12: 5). Billy Elliot and Evelyn live this out in different ways—as each of us does—according to the hidden designs and loving tangles of Providence. With

Evelyn there is her increasing immersion in the ocean of light and the gradual translation of the seat of her identity into the divinizing humanity of God in Christ. In the case of Billy, we recall the panel-member's recognition of the embers of his latent talent and the way grace building on nature displays itself in the powerful final scene when we ourselves are caught up in Billy's self-forgetful release into that soaring arc of muscled grace and beauty in *Swan Lake*. We saw Billy's father healed by this beauty, in the sense that a man who is shackled by decades of unshed tears is able to cry, if only for a few moments. With beauty comes hope.

When we are no longer objects of our own awareness, when we are un-selfed of the isolated self and no longer the goal of our own contemplative realization, we are more effective servants of the Master, laborers in the Lord's vineyard, and not the Lord of the harvest. This comes as a huge relief. Burdens we might not even know we carry drop away when we are not employing a technique to make them drop on command.

In reactive mind, and to a lesser extent in receptive mind as well, our contemplative project (ourselves) is held hostage by our fascination with it. This had a modest place when we were getting off to a start in response to an inner awakening or longing. It generated motivation, dedication, and enthusiasm (despite periods of boredom, falling by the wayside, or even a sense of falling apart at the seams). When we remain the focus of our contemplative project, however, what previously carried us along becomes a heavy burden to bear. In *On Watchfulness and Holiness*, St. Hesychios laments this very sort of thing: "A donkey going round and round in a mill cannot step out of the circle to which it is tethered. . . . With its inner eyes blinded, it cannot perceive the holiness or the radiant light of Jesus."[23] Centuries later, St. John of the Cross offers a similar observation, "The soul that journeys to God, but does not shake off its cares and quiet its appetites [grasping, clinging desire], is like one who drags a cart uphill."[24] Fascinated by our own contemplative realization, we remain tethered, moving constantly but going nowhere. But when the flower of awareness opens, we are relieved of the burden of ourselves as objects of our spiritual programs.

We Are All One

When the flower of awareness blossoms, breaking open into mindstream, we both embody and body forth our witness to the fact that we sit in silence at one with the entire world; there is a great, unmediated unity, a solidarity, a grounding union in the groundless ground of God in whom "we live and move and have our being" (Acts 17:28). In reactive mind, and more so in receptive mind, we might have had "sitting for the entire world, for every living being" as the grace-inspired intention we brought to practice. But in luminous mind, there is a grounding, differentiating union: we are all one in God in such a way that we manifest more fully what we as particular creatures are created to be. This arabesque of creation is only possible because of our creative union in the creating ground of God.

Recall how a child does not realize that playing peekaboo is funny until the child is old enough to develop "object permanence," the understanding that we are still present even if the child cannot see us hiding behind the sofa. Something analogous takes place in the spiritual life. Some have called it "subject permanence." It is a living sense that we are all of a piece. When this realization is permanently abiding we have crossed a development threshold: subject permanence. We may feel separated from others, and from a camera's point of view we are separate from one another. But for the single eye of the flower of awareness *we are one and have always been one*. But the "who" of who we are remains. Indeed, all creation maintains its own spectacular particularity. Only our purchase of the deceitful clutter of inner noise can convince us otherwise.

No longer the object of our own private scrutiny, luminous mind intuitively realizes this differentiating union— the more we see though the illusion of separation from God, the more fully created we are. Out of this realization emerges the flower of awareness. Its precious, pollen-painted petals of mind are a sanctuary of the most eloquent emptiness. We perceive the other and suddenly they are un-othered in the silent flow of the givingness of being.

Language fails us as it falls into the caverns of wordlessness only to arise like the phoenix singing of the Word made flesh (Jn 1:14). To perceive the truth of things requires our perception that, as we have heard St. Alphonsus Liguori and countless others say in so many words, "All there is, is God." Our gradual realization of this in the span of years we are given embodies and bodies forth the fullness of being both creature and the caring custodian of all beings (Gen 1:26). We listened to Howard Thurman bend his words to express something quite similar: "I hear His Voice in my own tongue and in accordance with the grain in my own wood. In that glorious and transcendent moment, it may easily seem to me that all there is, is God."[25] It is difficult for the grasping hands of our concepts to reach far into the silent land before language loses its bearings. In his *Homilies on the Song of Songs*, St. Gregory of Nyssa likens our conceptual insights to dew, "drops of the night": "It is impossible for a person entering the inner part of the sanctuary of the invisible to meet a drenching torrent of knowledge. Rather one must be content, if by a few obscure insights, truth bedews one's knowledge: these spiritual drops flow from the locks of the saints and the bearers of the divine."[26]

When we begin, habitually or even only occasionally, to encounter others not as *objects* but as *subjects*, while remaining created beings in all their glorious particularity, this is subject permanence. It arises from the Creator's loving design that makes each of us both creative and creating. Evagrius attempts to give voice to this subject permanence when he says, "A monk is someone who considers himself one with all because he seems constantly to see himself in everyone."[27]

When the flower of awareness emerges from luminous mind, we encounter others interiorly as our very selves, as though we are right up inside their skin, a reverent witness of the sacred brokenness of their life stories shining with generous beauty. When this happens on a more or less regular basis, it marks the emergence of a great realization that unothers the other. "For as in one body we have many parts, and all the parts do not have the same function, so we, though many, are one body in Christ and individually parts of one another" (Rom 12:4–5).

The emergence of object permanence in very young children indicates normal psychological development; subject permanence, by the grace of God seeing the other not as an object but as the sheer givingness of being is natural spiritual development. Jesus' prayer to the Father is as much a declaration of the simple suchness of life as it is a supplication: "May they be one, as You, Father, are in Me, and I am in You. May they also be one in Us" (Jn 17:21).

We Stop Comparing Ourselves with Others

In reactive mind, and to a lesser extent in receptive mind, we meet a highly conditioned, socially sanctioned tendency to look around and compare ourselves with others on the contemplative path. They are surely doing it better than we are: "Just look at them. They're so calm." The reactive mind, whether obsessively, subtly, or worse, subconsciously, measures its steady advance in contemplation against what it has decided (based on nothing) the progress of others must certainly be. This enables reactive mind to do two things at once: remain the sole arbiter of its own progress (however illusory) and at the same time keep a close eye on what others are up to. For receptive mind, there is much less concern about progress. It is drawn to the vastness (God, according to the *Cloud* author) we perceive by looking over the shoulders of distraction. For luminous mind, comparing our progress with that of others is no longer a concern. Moreover, the innate wisdom of luminous mind realizes that progress need not feel like progress. So there really isn't any progress or lack of progress for us to watch. In his *Spiritual Letters*, the early twentieth-century Benedictine monk John Chapman says, "Progress will mean becoming more and more indifferent as to what state we are in. . . . We must not worry about perfection even; simply be what God enables us to be at this moment."

Chapman further advises, "Look upon it as a temptation to think about your state. . . . There is a danger of devout people living for themselves instead of for others.[28]

As for comparing ourselves with others, the entire house of cards collapses.

SPECIAL CHALLENGES

There is a special challenge for luminous mind: not to cling, not even to enlightenment—the flower of awareness. We see the importance of non-clinging in both the teaching and example of Jesus. In his Letter to the Philippians, St. Paul observes that Jesus did not cling to His equality with God, "Who, though he was in the form of God, did not regard equality with God something that could be grasped. Rather he emptied himself and took the form of a slave" (Phil 2:6–7). Jesus' equality with God could not be realized by means of clinging.

Jesus likewise teaches his non-clinging to Mary Magdalene. Mary discovers that the stone had been rolled away from Jesus' tomb. She runs home to tell Peter and the disciple whom Jesus loved (according to ancient tradition, John the Evangelist) that the Lord's body was gone. Peter and John race to the tomb. They depart, but Mary stays behind. Suddenly a man, whom Mary takes to be a gardener, calls her by name, "Mary." Only then—when he calls her by her name—does she immediately recognize him as the Risen Lord. Jesus begins to teach. "Do not cling to me—*noli me tangere*" (Jn 20:17). We can see that Jesus both models (Phil 2:6–7) and teaches (Jn 20:17) the importance of not clinging to any realization of the Divine. The Flemish Beguine Hadewijch of Brabant (thirteenth century) astutely observes: "We do not find it written anywhere that Christ ever, in his entire life, had recourse to his Father or his omnipotent Nature to obtain joy and repose. He never gave himself any satisfaction, but continually undertook new labors from the beginning of his life to the end."[29] Hadewijch provides us with a very useful teaching: Jesus never took refuge, never clung to the divine nature in order to avoid the struggles of the human condition. Because Jesus did not avoid them but accepted them, these very struggles, like death itself, are no longer obstacles but doorways for those who walk by faith and not by sight (2 Cor 5:7).

Remember the Songs of the Suffering Servant from the prophet Isaiah, "Yet ours were the infirmities he bore, ours the sufferings he suffered" (Is 53:4). Centuries later we hear echoes in the Letter to the Hebrews, "We have in Christ Jesus a high priest who is no stranger to human weakness, but one who has been tried in every way just as we are tried, yet without sin. . . . Jesus is able to deal patiently with the ignorant and with those who have strayed; for he himself is beset by weakness" (Heb 4:15; 5:2).

Naïve presumptions still whisper from behind trees. Despite their intimate relationship Adam hides from Yahweh behind the trees, ashamed of his own newly discovered nakedness. Adam was always naked before God. The difference now is that Adam's nakedness is an occasion of shame from which emerge his famous stories of blame (Gen 3:10). These shackles of shame exist only in our minds along with the endless stream of inner chatter they generate.

We continue to purchase this illusion, adapted to our own unique circumstances. This illusion speaks in one hundred thousand splintered tongues: "the blossoming of the flower of awareness means that our life-issues, our personal struggles and strife are somehow left behind if we are just silent enough." Lots of luck. If we find ourselves taken in by this, it is clear that we yet cling to contemplative practice *as a strategy* to acquire something (very often we know not quite what). It is a subtly deceiving strategy that tells us that the practice of contemplation will remove the pain, the boredom, and inconvenience (often considerable) of the daily circumstances of our lives as they happen to be *right now*. Even luminous mind, though it knows better, will attempt to cling to not clinging, attempt to cling to this "green and pleasant land" that eschews all clinging.

When human longing is consummated by the silence of God, we are fully created as self-forgetful vehicles of compassion. Life will continue to involve pain, struggle, and duress. But pain, *decluttered* of the biting and chewing chatter that says life should be other than it is at this very moment, is very good practice, even if there is still a good deal of biting, chewing chatter involved. Everything that appears in awareness is the best possible practice there is. This includes the ordeals of cancer, humiliation addiction, our loss of hearing or sight, our depression, our ALS, or Alzheimer's. What changes is *how we perceive, respond to, and live out* our most challenging struggles and failures—life circumstances as they happen to be. For these are spokes leading into the same hub of Light (Jn 8:12) as faith, hope, love, joy, reverence, or simplicity. The realization that both simple joy and splinters failure are vehicles of light is the fruit of the life-long work of the integration of what we loathe most about ourselves, resent most in others, and find most intolerable about our own misshapen lives, even as we try to live them out as best we can. The integration of all this happens by means of the "light that shines in darkness, a light that darkness cannot overpower" (Jn 1:15). This is the mystery we call God, for whom night is as bright as day: "Even the dark is not dark to you; the night is as bright as the day: for dark and light are the same to you" (Ps 139:2). We all have our own preferences as to what each day should bring; the decluttered, non-clinging, luminous mind perceives that despair and delight reveal the very same Light. Now we hear harmony where once we heard only discord.

CONCLUSION

These distinctions among reactive mind, receptive mind, and luminous mind should not be seen as *anything but labels* that serve a limited purpose on an unchartable terrain. They are not suggested as clearly delineated stages to help us locate ourselves on a map. There is a great deal of fluidity, and maps are not especially fond of fluidity. What we have presented are the simplest of offerings in the hope of shedding light upon some of the challenges that are often our daily bread. They are mere signposts on a pathless path.

PART III

SIX

Our Uninvited Guests

Depression and Its Friends

A man of sorrows and acquainted with grief.
——Isaiah 53:3

You shall not fear the terrors of the night nor the
arrows that fly by day.
——Psalm 91:5

My only friend is darkness.
——Psalm 88:19

INTRODUCTION: SQUATTER'S RIGHTS

There has been a lot of talk in the last several years about how
meditative disciplines, such as mindfulness meditation, help
free us from the shackles of depression and anxiety (the two
are often joined at the hip). For the sake of simplicity I will use
the term "depression" here to include both depression and its
friends, such as anxiety, dark thoughts, poor sleep, nausea, and
loss of appetite. Even the most cosmetic forms of contemplative
practice can be an enormous help in treating and relieving the

symptoms of depression. An impressive body of sound scientific research backs this up.[1] The practice of contemplation can be a natural and lasting treatment for depression (chronic or acute) and its significant other, anxiety. As the author of *The Cloud of Unknowing* says, "The work of contemplation will have a favorable effect on the body as well as the soul of anybody who practices it."[2]

This is wonderful news. However, what if we are seasoned contemplatives and continue to meet depression, even serious depression? Not only does our depression come and go for varying lengths of time, but it can come and *refuse to budge*. Next thing we know depression and its friends have claimed squatter's rights in our lives. These include highly habituated thought patterns such as harsh judgments against ourselves, especially self-loathing; the communion of inner solitude curdling into suffocating isolation; feelings of being cut off; having difficulty receiving the love of others—including God's unconditional love; self-medicating; poor appetite; inconsistent patterns of sleep; dark thoughts of every sort. The routine, semipermanent, or even permanent presence of these uninvited guests can leave contemplatives feeling like pious frauds. After all, the literature says that meditation is supposed to pry loose depression's grip. Yet for some reason our contemplative practice does not obey the literature. As a result, we consider ourselves contemplative failures. This makes matters worse as we try to keep it all hidden in order to avoid the social stigma that continues to attach to something that is called a "mental illness." It would be far better for us say with conviction, "depression is a factor in my inner weather." Instead we purchase the stigma and consume it like some forbidden fruit and feel we need to hide. Hiding did not work for Adam and Eve (Gen 3:8) and it will not work for us. It only adds weight to what is already burdensome. According to the author of the *Cloud* we should be prepared for all this, and he encourages us not to be derailed by the fact that it is happening. He says in his *Letter of Private Direction*, "And do not be dismayed by any disquieting fear, though the fiend should come, as indeed he will, bringing sudden panic, banging and beating on the walls of your house."[3]

While we clearly prefer to be relieved of this burden, sometimes this simply does not happen. If it seems that depression is a frequent pattern of our inner weather, semipermanently or for such very long stretches of time as to seem permanent, it is important for us to get to know our depression in intimate detail rather than futilely insist that it go away. The contemplative skill needed is the same as it is for every other situation: allow it to be present simply because it happens to be present. Knowing directly and intimately the unique contours of our depression (not simply knowing about it) can let in the slightest bit of fresh air that has never been breathed before. Even if depression does not loosen its grip, the skills of self-knowledge and inner vigilance remain life-giving.

Everyone's depression is different. We all have different personal stories, genetic packages, and life histories. We are all the same in radically unique ways. For some it's a matter of genetics; we are prone to depression because the brain does not produce sufficient quantities of serotonin, norepinephrine, dopamine, GABA, and so on. Perhaps we've struggled with depression most of our lives, or perhaps somewhere in our journey a traumatic event has "flicked on the genetic switch," and there is no obvious way to flick it back off. Others may have self-medicated themselves onto the alcoholism spectrum in an attempt to treat their life-pain, their depression. The problem here is that eventually alcohol increases both the anxiety and depression it once promised to relieve. The struggle with depression is worsened by the social stigma that is still very much attached to it. This can increase the shame or self-loathing that often feeds the depression. This stigma is reinforced by health professionals who want to help us. They tell us we have a "disorder" and may even read us something from the DSM (*Diagnostic and Statistical Manual of Mental Disorders*—the ultimate authority in the psychiatric and legal professions). In the medical world "disorder" is a technical term that simply means medical professionals do not know the origins of the condition (in contrast to a disease). But in standard English the word "disorder" is stronger, more indicting, and a bit judgmental: not only are we depressed but there is also something about us that is messy or untidy and needs to be cleaned up. Hence, in addition to depression we also feel embarrassed or ashamed that we are bad emotional housekeepers on top of everything else that is apparently wrong with us. By clinging to their own technical jargon instead of translating it into standard English, medical professionals unwittingly add extra weight to what we already find difficult to bear.

In a challenging poem, "Pediatric Suicide," Franz Wright objects strongly to being defined by the DMS, or perhaps he is resisting his own tendency to allow himself to be labeled with terms such as "disorder" or "diagnosis":

> Being who you are is not a disorder
> Being unloved is not a psychiatric disorder.
> I can't find being born in a diagnostic manual.[4]

People who have depression know that there remains some hidden, essential something that cannot be shoehorned into the narrow shoes of a definition that comes out of a manual. No matter the behaviors, feelings, or moods we might present, no diagnostic term can pin down the *who* of who we are. In a journal entry dated August 26, 2004, Wendell Miles writes, "Don't minimize my life, people. Thoughts, desires for knowledge, inner peace: my whole life has been in these pursuits. Some genetics are probably my worst enemy, some environmental factors. Please do not put me in a category."[5]

Depression is not just another afflictive thought. It is more like the low barometric pressure of a weather system that moves in. Sometimes it remains for only a short time before it moves on; sometimes depression settles in and stays for longer than we could ever have imagined. It can even become a permanent, uninvited guest in our home. Others may live with a more or less permanent, low- or medium-grade depression and then experience an even heavier depression that hangs around as long as it likes until it lifts and we return to the normal depression that we have long grown accustomed to. There are as many depressions as there are people suffering from them. From the perspective of the practice of contemplation, it is more a question of knowing what our inner climate is than knowing whether or not the DSM has a convenient label for it.

Depression is not in itself an afflictive thought, but depression brings along with it many of its sinister pals that are deeply afflictive. We listed some of these earlier: harsh judgments against ourselves, especially self-loathing; experiencing the communion of inner solitude turning into feelings of isolation; the sense of being cut off; difficulty or even fear of receiving the love others have for us— including God's unconditional love; self-medicating; nausea; poor appetite; irregularity in personal hygiene; inconsistent patterns of sleep; dark thoughts of every sort imaginable. For others depression is likewise present, but somewhat better behaved than the afflictions just described.

Among the most challenging aspects of the struggle with depression is the *struggling itself.* Struggling is like thrashing in quicksand. We sink quickly. If depression has set up house in our home, then in addition to the interior skills of self-knowledge and inner vigilance, depression itself simply becomes our contemplative practice. We may struggle against accepting depression as practice, but both the struggle against the depression and giving up in despair are results of inner chatter. When, through the practice of contemplation, inner stillness emerges, depression holds out possibilities we never dreamt of *even when depression remains.*

The purpose of this chapter is to suggest that the contemplative who has depression as a regular, uninvited guest can play a vitally important *intercessory role* for others who have the same struggle but who have no contemplative practice to turn to. A profound inner awakening can emerge even in the midst of depression. This awakening does not necessarily mean that depression goes away. Depression is still a wounding of sorts that leaves us exposed to the jagged edges of the mind. Yet out of this wound a flower blossoms—the flower of awareness. Even as it resists treatment, depression can give birth to many beautiful children: deep insight into oneself as well as other people; profound compassion for all, especially the suffering; the ability to see straight through this uninvited guest who has moved in long enough to claim squatter's rights. Just like any affliction, depression can become a place of intercession and solidarity with others. We become a bridge for all those who have no bridge.

JAGGED EDGES OF THE MIND

For some reason we think that in order to move forward, there must be so much light that we see the road ahead of us lit up for miles and miles ahead. This happens only very rarely. Thankfully, it is not necessary to see so far ahead into the future. The future is often murky no matter the hope we have for it. Even if we do not see the way, we yet move forward. Not very much light is required. When driving at night, we see very little of the road ahead; the headlights illuminate the road for only so many yards and the night keeps all the rest as black as pitch. But those several yards that are illumined are sufficient. As we move forward, without knowing the way, the headlights light up just enough road for us to see. It really is not very much light. But just enough is more than enough. This light, little though it is, is a "light that shines in the darkness; a light that darkness cannot over power" (Jn 1:5). The light in inner chaos and despair (the two often seem identical) shines even when inner chaos and despair remain and serve as its vehicle. Yes, it is darkness, but paradoxically "a darkness all of light."[6] The Psalmist sings this same paradox in Psalm 139:12:

> Darkness is not dark for you
> And night shines as the day.
> Darkness and light are but one.

The contemplative life is bejeweled with paradox: darkness that is at the same time light; darkness and light are one; "luminous darkness," as St. Gregory of Nyssa called it. Paradox has a specific function. It brings the thinking (discursive) mind to stillness.

There is no such thing as light that is at the time darkness. This stillness is a home for everybody—even for those with chronic, rattling depression that will not go away as the meditation therapists say it will. In all depression there is some light. Insofar as we are aware of depression, there is something within us that is free of depression; otherwise we could not be aware of it. The awareness itself does not necessarily lift our depression, though it seems to for many. But that small opening of awareness provides just enough light to illuminate the road, even if it is only a question of several yards, allowing us to keep moving forward without knowing what lies just ahead. As we drive along the road, no matter its twists and turns, the headlights light up just as much road as necessary, constantly revealing new patches of the road ahead.

Depression can help us stay anchored in the present moment; for it limits us to coping with getting through the day one step at a time, one half-hour at a time—whatever it takes. This is actually the only dosage life comes in: one step at a time (one day at a time can sometimes seem over-ambitious). The union of attention and breath keeps us where our bodies are and requires no abundance of light.

People who have depression often feel they have no voice of their own; it has been stolen by diagnoses and treatment protocols. In what follows we allow such people to have a voice. They speak of what the practice of contemplation is like in the midst of depression that will not budge. Whether their practice is in reactive mind, receptive mind, or luminous mind, they have a voice!

BLACK HOURS OF ENDLESS NIGHTS—MILLICENT

I long to escape from the paralysis of the day's mental fog and jump into the arms of sleep. Yet, every night I dread climbing into bed. Despite the medication I am on, the friendship that sleep promises always betrays me just as every friend I remember having in school, departed with no good-bye: her father was suddenly transferred; the friend changed schools—there was always some reason.

At night I am more vulnerable to the vultures that see my mind as, if not carrion, then easy prey. I remembered a line from the Bible, "You shall not fear the terrors of the night, nor the arrows that fly by day" (Ps 91:5). I am a Christian and am inspired by the way Jesus treated those on the margins. It is obvious in the New Testament that, in the eyes of Jesus, those who don't count *count*. Both as a woman and as someone who feels very much on the margins of life, I feel I matter to Jesus who says he is "the way, the truth, and the life" (Jn 14:6). I long to be looked at by Jesus.

When I was young, my paternal grandmother, who seemed to understand me—if not, she certainly liked me—gave me a cross. She said, "Millicent, darling, this is a hand cross. Hold it tight in your hand whenever you feel anxious or upset." It fit perfectly in my hand. The cross lay across my palm, and the arms of the cross fit just where my thumb joined the rest of my hand and the other arm lay between my index finger and the middle finger beneath it. The hand cross didn't make the depression go away, but it gave me something physical to hold on to and focus on. Eventually this wooden hand cross would walk me like a pilgrim into a few hours' sleep.

I cannot remember the last time I slept soundly for more than a few hours at a time. About the only time when depression loosens its vice is when I get out of the bed in the morning and shower. I remember years ago when I learned

Tai Chi. One of our warm-up exercises had us all vigorously patting up and down the sides of our arms and legs. I felt wide awake and could feel vital energy rising in my body. I noticed that other people's faces suddenly had a rosy color. This exercise was called "raising the *Chi*." I don't do Tai Chi anymore because it left me facing my own thoughts which I simply could not bear in my present state. But I remember this exercise every time I shower. Though certainly less vigorous, the movements are practically the same when showering. I wear exfoliating gloves and when I apply the shower gel I finish washing by patting up and down my arms and legs just like I did during Tai Chi. I feel invigorated. The energy of the *Chi* rises. My spirits do lift for a while, and I say to myself, the depression is lifting, which it is. But only for 20 minutes or so. But in this brief period of time I breathe in and out air and light. Then the fatigue of depression soon returns. I leave the house and join friends for morning coffee and scones. They've all been up since dawn exercising, kick boxing, and lifting weights. The only weight I lift is the weight of my own body as I try to get out of the bed. I should say, *my friends* have coffee. I have hot water with lemon or perhaps chamomile or peppermint tea. A cup of coffee would set off the anxiety two hours before the anxiety sets itself off. The anxiety builds and builds until it begins to roar and pound like the Tin Man's hollow chest in *The Wizard of Oz*. Inevitably a friend will ask me, "How did you sleep?" I respond, "Oh, like a baby." This is just to dodge the question. If I answered the question truthfully, "How did you sleep?" I'd respond, "I slept like a baby. I woke up every couple of hours crying." It's a fairly well-known joke, but much of the time this is the God's honest truth.

Millicent had debilitating depression on and off for decades. She is now in her late fifties. She didn't know what the word meant, much less that it applied to her, until she went off to university and learned about depression in a psychology class. Once, when she was home for Christmas break, she told her parents, "I think I might have serious depression." Her parents replied that depression was a form of self-indulgence. It would go away if she spent more time being grateful for the things she had that less fortunate people didn't. Millicent said to herself, "But I *am* grateful for the things I have but I still have depression." She never discussed it again with her parents, and they forgot that the conversation, such as it was, ever took place.

When I was young my father had to drop me off at school early twice a week so that he could get to some meeting (it was thirty years before I discovered he was going to AA meetings). The school doors were not open yet. The only place to go was the church. There were always a few other

students in there too. I loved going in there at that hour.
The nuns were still chanting Lauds [morning prayer].
I had never heard or seen anything like it. Their voices
were lilting. Their harmonies revealed a depth-dimension
to life itself, as though what we can perceive with our senses
was only scratching the surface. It was so calming. I never
wanted it to end.

Millicent did experience moments of relief no matter how
brief: the nuns' chanting and the hand cross given to her by
her grandmother.

Millicent liked to paint her toenails. She recalls,

I was all balled up in the very large chair in my room getting
ready to paint my toenails. All balled up painting my nails
introduced me to a different dimension of my mind that
was free of all the incessant noise in my head. I don't know
if it was the centeredness I felt due to the position of my
body or to the self-forgetfulness that happens accidentally,
such as concentrating in order to apply the tip of the brush
to each toenail—perhaps the combination—there suddenly opened both within me and around me a quiet center
that was untouched by the noise of my inner chaos. There
was a circle of sunlight around my feet. A patch of light
with enough space to live in. It didn't last long but its mark
is permanent. In the midst of depression there is a spacious
corner of light.

This realization marked a turning point in Millicent's life. Depression is present. Sleep (or the lack of it) is still an ordeal, just as it was for the late Victorian poet and Jesuit priest Gerard Manley Hopkins (1844–1889). A man of deep and anguished prayer, in his poem "I Wake and Feel" he wrote of the black hours of sleep:

> I wake and feel the fell of dark, not day.
> What hours, O what black hours we have spent
> This night! what sights you, heart, saw, ways you went!
> And more must, in yet longer light's delay.[7]

Millicent knows all too well these black hours of endless nights.

But there is something that underlies Millicent's depression. It is a bit like what Franny Glass experiences in J. D. Salinger's novella, *Franny*. Franny is having lunch at a restaurant with her tediously self-centered and inattentive boyfriend, Lane. Suddenly there is a splash of sunlight where Franny's attention can rest. "Franny was staring at the little blotch of sunshine with a special intensity, as if she were considering lying down in it."[8] Like Millicent, Franny feels as if she is not permitted to have a voice of her own. Franny is undergoing some sort of breakdown. Unlike Franny, Millicent has lived most of her life in a state of breakdown. But the emergence of even a small splash of light creates enough space for each of them to *be*—a space wide enough to stretch out in.

Millicent stumbled onto silent prayer—a way of just being still before God—without benefit of instruction. The physical stillness, centeredness, and concentration of painting her toenails suddenly revealed a circle of silence within her. Here she could just be, despite the roaring, inner chaos within her. Millicent had seen this world of inner silence before. Decades earlier, the nuns' chanting had opened up another dimension of life, not separate from yet still free of her life of depression and inner chaos.

In a memoir of his own descent into crippling depression, the American author William Styron writes: "Depression is a disorder [*sic*] of mood, so mysteriously painful and elusive in the way it becomes known to the self . . . so as to verge close to being beyond description. It remains nearly incomprehensible to those who have not experienced it in its extreme mode."[9]

Styron reminds us that the descent into depression is a descent into mystery, a mystery incomprehensible to those who have not themselves driven on this dimly lit road. Millicent teaches us that her descent into depression does not have the final word on a life rich in meaning. Her discovery of inner silence in the presence of the inner noise of depression has bestowed meaning and purpose on her life. As she put it,

In these small patches I discover that the world is a place where I belong and am welcomed by the "the love of God that comes to us in Christ Jesus" (Rom 8:39). It does not matter (despite my preference) that "my only friend is darkness" (Ps 88:19). Darkness itself, even this disabling darkness, is a vehicle of a small space of light and air. My role in life is a humble one and in the eyes of many it is inadequate in every direction. But because of this growing inner space of light-filled air I can breathe and *be*. I am at home in the universe. I have a role in the universe.

HOPE AND ABANDONMENT—BRENDAN

I had placed so much hope in the claim that meditation would get rid of the depression I have had for the better part of twenty-five years. This is what the retreat director we had one year said it would do, among other promises he made that never panned out. I gave myself completely to this way of silent prayer and saw how it was described by many of the ancient monastic sources in our tradition. It appealed to something deep within me, something deeper than my thoughts and feelings went. Even to this day, even after years of practicing this way of praying by being still before God, despite the chaos and turmoil within, I do not understand my attraction. It is simply the call of being, or as the Psalms put it, "Deep calling unto deep in the roar of your waters" (Ps 42:7). But the depression did not go away. I could certainly identify with something about these depths even in the midst of depression's own sort of roar. While I think the compass of my own silence always found true North, some pole star that would keep me on path, the roar was the roar of inner chaos, which I doubt is what the Psalmist had in mind when he said, "in the roar of your waters (Ps 42:7)."

My depression set in about four years after I entered the monastery. This is about the time when a monk, still relatively new to the life, is in the early part of his discernment of whether to make a life-long commitment to the place and the people in it or to leave the monastery. I had discussed the depression with those monks whose job it was to introduce me to the monastic life and be there for support during a crisis, and prevent, insofar as possible, a young monk from using the monastic life to hide from himself. As far as I could tell, the options for doing this were limited to either using our daily work as a defense against the necessity of self-knowledge or getting caught up in the politics of the monastery. From what I could see, this was pretty easy to do.

These monks (the formation team), both as a group and individually, were very encouraging. While I thought the depression was a clear sign from God that I did not have a vocation, they said this is not always the case and that unless I freely wanted to leave, they would encourage me to stay. They assured me that if I were meant to leave the monastery, either they would notice certain signs or the very walls would shout, "Get out!" Otherwise I was free and welcome to stay. I felt very encouraged by this, and it really helped keep me going. "But," I said, "does the Abbot know?"

They looked at one another until finally the monk who was immediately in charge of me, the Junior Master, said, "I don't think so unless you told him. What you say to us in confidence remains in confidence." I said, "I think the Abbot should know." "Well, Brother Brendan," the Junior Master said, "make an appointment with him. But he won't say anything different." I had the sense that they were not as alarmed about me as I was.

I knocked on Abbot Adrian's door and got an enthusiastic, "Come in." I entered. He got up, came around his desk, and aimed himself right at me. As he approached he opened his arms ("he's got quite a wing span," I said to myself) and gave me a reassuring embrace, "Brother Brendan, it's great to see you. It's been a while since we've had a chat."

We sat down. There was long silence.

I thought he would start the conversation and I think he presumed I was going to start talking. Finally, he said, "So what's up?" I said, "I've been pretty depressed for a long time now and I'm wondering if this means I don't have a vocation and should leave the monastery." He nodded, trying to be understanding, but he didn't look the slightest bit alarmed. His expression was a bit curious. He looked as though I'd just said, "1 + 1 = 2." The Abbot asked, "Do you want to leave?" I said, "No." Abbot Adrian asked, "Then why do you think you should leave?" "Because I'm depressed, like I just said."

The Abbot leaned back in his chair and said, "Brother Brendan, if everybody around here left because they struggled with depression, we'd have closed the place down ages ago. Medication works for some of the monks who have depression. Then there are others who tell me that medication is of little help and that they might as well be chewing gum. I think you should consider trying medication, just to see if you get some relief. Have a word with the doctor next week. It's completely up to you. But frankly, I myself get very little relief from the various meds he's tried me on. Everybody is different."

I nearly fell out of the chair. I said, "You get depressed?" "Well, yes, don't look so surprised. Why do you think I don't make it down for Vigils at 3:30 half the time? With depression, sleep often eludes me. For me it's the heavy fatigue from poor sleep that's often more difficult than low mood. It comes and goes. But, as I said, everybody is different. For some reason we think that because something in our lives is a burden to bear, this means we have taken a wrong turn somewhere. It's not that simple, Brother Brendan. It's just not that simple. If I were you, I'd get to know the silence of your heart as well as you know your depression. The two are not the polar opposites you take them to be."

The Abbot's words address something which confounds most of us. If life hurts, something is wrong with life, and we must change it so that it does not hurt. Well, that is wonderful if it happens to work. Obviously, we are not speaking of social and personal injustices that cry out for the healing embrace of truth, justice, and reconciliation. But even here there are no guarantees. We are speaking more directly of how our minds meet conflict with either rejection or flight. If the spiritual life leads to difficulty, there must be something wrong with our path. In his *Letters to a Young Poet*, Rainer Maria Rilke writes, "The tasks that have been entrusted to us are often difficult. Almost everything that matters is difficult, and everything matters."[10] Rilke suggests that we adopt a different attitude to difficulty. Depression is such a difficulty. We should consider the difficulty of depression as though it were something *entrusted* to us. What does this do? It changes our relationship with depression. When we are entrusted with something we must exercise stewardship of it. At the very least our stewardship of depression that will not budge requires that we accept it. When we accept what we resist, things change. Exercising stewardship of our depression gives us the liberating space to stop thrashing in the quicksand of this burden of sadness. When we stop thrashing in quicksand, the quicksand will stop swallowing us alive. Letting be what we are entrusted with loosens depression's grip even if it does not go away. Again, the contemplative maxim: we let be whatever is simply because it is. Other actions proceed from this.

Brendan kept with his practice of being still in the midst of whatever winds were blowing.

> I go for long stretches of feeling mainly abandoned. But increasingly I do not feel alone when I am abandoned. I think of Jesus' cry of abandonment from the cross: "My God, my God, why have you abandoned me?" (Ps 22:2). According to the Gospels Jesus died soon after that. But I wonder if Jesus meant to stop there. When we were studying the Gospels, I can remember our professor saying that in the ancient world, to recite the first line of a Psalm implied the entirety of the Psalm. Maybe Jesus intended to recite the entire Psalm but was too weak after receiving thirty lashes and then nailed to a cross along with the others. Halfway through this Psalm the mood changes from despair to praise, confidence, and hope:

> Then I will proclaim your name to the assembly;
> in the community I will praise you:
> You who fear the Lord, give praise!
> All descendants of Jacob, give honor;
> show reverence, all descendants of Israel!

For God has not spurned or disdained
the misery of this poor wretch,
Did not turn away from me,
but heard me when I cried out . . .

The poor will eat their fill;
those who seek the Lord will offer praise.
May your hearts enjoy life forever! (Ps 22:23–27)

The Psalm continues along these lines until the end. This
Psalm starts out with despair and feelings of abandonment
but ends in joy, hope, and praise!

Brendan remembered what the Abbot had said, "Get to
know the silence of your heart as well as you know your depression. The two are not the polar opposites you take them to be."
Brendan remembered how the retreat director taught the community about silent meditation. In fact, Brendan had continued
this contemplative practice. A number of other monks gathered a
couple of times during the day to spend a half-hour or so praying
by simply *being*. Insofar as they were, they were prayer. Brendan
never missed. In his head were turbulence, fog, and sharp edges.
Those who do not know this inner state for themselves cannot
possibly imagine it. Again, as Gerard Manley Hopkins, well
acquainted with depression in his own life, expresses it:

No worst, there is none. Pitched past pitch of grief,
More pangs will, schooled at forepangs, wilder wring.

Comforter, where, where is your comforting? . . .

O the mind, mind has mountains; cliffs of fall

Frightful, sheer, no-man-fathomed.[11]

The precipices of our minds are not the final word, however. As deeply penetrating as the "pitch of grief" and the storms of turbulence are, like any mood or cluster of thoughts they do not go as deeply as we go. We can discover these depths, live out of them, be for others out of them even when depression and its friends have claimed squatter's rights in our lives. Brendan came to see this for himself and how to live for others out of his depression.

Over the years Brendan spoke less of being depressed. He might say, "I have depression" or "depression is present." But we could not in truth equate "self" with depression. He was much more receptive to the presence of depression. Instead of bouncing off or thrashing against depression he simply allowed it to be there, as though entrusted with this difficulty, but without demanding that it go away if it wasn't going away, which it usually didn't. One day Brendan tried to share this liberating transition to a brother monk. The monk didn't have the foggiest idea of what Brendan was talking about and said, "Wow! You sound really depressed. You know, the doctor comes here once a week. He's very understanding. You can talk to him about anything." Brendan rolled his eyes and returned to what he was doing. Depression maintained its heaviness, but Brendan had realized for himself that depression does not go as deeply as he goes. The label of depression does not adhere to identity.

Now on the other side of middle age, Brendan says,

> People often say that I am very gifted just because I have a decent voice for singing and know what I'm doing in the kitchen. Yes, I have an eye for simple ways of helping the monks in the infirmary feel better and less frightened. However, the skills I admit to being grateful for are the ability to get out of bed each morning and stay out of bed and to keep putting one foot in front of the other. If I can do that, I've got the day. But being by *still* in the midst of depression, whether I am sitting in silent prayer or going about my various chores, I experience a great solidarity with all people, especially with those who have depression and see no way out. "There is no way *out*," I would tell them. "The way out is the way *in*." Only then can we step out of what we take to be ourselves into a Love that embraces both life and death. Over the decades depression has taught me never to stray far from my breath. In this hidden way I intercede for others simply by way of stillness and breath. I am a rudder for the countless people who sail without a rudder of their own.

St. Augustine speaks movingly of the necessity of trial or temptation (testing). In his *Commentary on Psalm 60*, he says, "During this earthly pilgrimage our life cannot be free from temptation, for none of us comes to self-knowledge except through the experience of temptation; nor can we be crowned until we have come through victorious; nor be victorious until we have been in battle; nor fight our battles unless we have an enemy and temptation to overcome."[12] St. Augustine, who himself was tried as any of us are tried, is convinced that there is nothing, no matter how defeating, that is beyond God's ability to use for our good.

THE WAVES ENCOMPASSED ME—JONAS

Jonas had always hoped that he could avoid the depression that had plagued his family for generations. In fact, he started his practice of contemplation as a sort of depression preventative.

It was not long, however, before he became deeply committed to this path for its own sake and not for how it might serve as a deterrent for depression. Jonas learned something life-giving about silence which the contemplative path revealed to him. "In silence I have discovered everything I hoped to discover in love. I have been fortunate enough to encounter both silence and love. To me they are one."

Jonas had never known depression until a certain traumatic event woke depression from its genetic slumber. The trigger took place at work. Jonas says,

I date my life according what took place before and after this event. A relatively new hire (Samuel) at work who reports to me filed a complaint against me with Human Resources. The letter accused me of being hostile, intolerant, an eavesdropper, out to get him from the first day he started work. I actually have very little to do with him on a day-to-day basis. What did happen?

I was reading an extensive report he wrote. The report was very well done in every way. But it did not take into account certain figures covering a five-year period. I asked him to stop by my office. I put it to him matter-of-factly and indicated that the incompleteness of the report was not his fault. The missing information had never been given to him in the first place. The data had to be taken into account, but it would require only a day or so to analyze the data and then create a new section of the report and cut and paste them in. That's it. The report was truly excellent, well organized, and well written, his analyses were fantastic. Samuel said, "But this will make my report late." "Well, yes," I said, "but that deadline was set by me. There is no problem in taking a couple of days to take account of the material that was not given to you. This was someone else's fault, Samuel, not yours. It's easy to correct." "It will still be late and it will make me look bad." Before I could say that it would not make him look bad, he was storming out of my office. That's it. But as I said earlier the letter accused me of being hostile towards him, intolerant, an eavesdropper, out to get him from the first day he started work. Well, the God's honest truth is that out of all the candidates for the position I chose him because he stood head and shoulders above other highly qualified applicants. I have dealt with letters such as these. Often there is at least a grain of truth to any given complaint. But not *one single thing* he said in his letter was true.

Human Resources emailed me the next day. The letter was attached. The email said I was to have no contact with this employee in any way. The email and attachment were copied to my immediate boss and to our CEO. When I read that letter it was as though a bomb had exploded in my face. I felt accused by Human Resources. I felt my job was on the line. I felt waves of anger come over me. There was an intense panic: I felt I was drowning; felt a desperate need to come up for air. But I felt trapped and unable to come up for air. I was trapped with no advocate and no place to turn. I was sweating and was very short of breath.

As a result of this traumatic event Jonas's life was flooded with depression. Medication tamed the intensity of the panic attacks. He was left with medium-grade chronic anxiety with occasional spikes. Jonas went through all the medications and got some partial relief from one of them. But ultimately, the depression was considered "treatment-resistant."

What Jonas had feared might happen to him did in fact happen. He received the dark inheritance that was part of his family's genetic estate. His sentiment was much what we read in the Book of Job (3:24–36). Job says,

> For sighing comes more readily to me than food.
>> and my groans well forth like water.
> For what I fear overtakes me,
>> and what I shrink from comes upon me.
> I have no peace nor ease;
>> I have no rest, for trouble comes!

Jonas said,

> The doctor says that despite the fact that my depression is resistant to treatment that I was considered to be "high-functioning." The only way anyone could get this impression would be if they simply watched me on a CCTV camera. Despite exercise and a healthy diet, each day remains a struggle to get through from dawn to dusk. Some days anger dominates; other days it's mental fog and lethargy. I am very easily overwhelmed. When the sense of being overwhelmed (the slightest thing can trigger it) hits me I feel as though I am drowning. I admit I have had thoughts of taking my life. But I have never attempted it

or plotted to do so. This is not due to anything courageous in me. Quite the opposite. I don't have the courage to take my own life. That's simply how I see it. Cowardice is not normally considered a virtue. But to be honest the main reason I am alive is due to love. Depression does not extinguish my ability to love my wife and children. Depression does, however, make it difficult for me to receive the love that is there. But the love I feel for my family is really what prevents me from any sort of self-harm.

It is worth noticing the refrains of anger and the sense of drowning in Jonas's ordeal. Many throughout history have likewise described their battles with depression with the language of anger and drowning. Thousands of years ago, the Psalmist wrote, "Like waters, terrors encompass me all day long; they encompass me on all sides" (Ps 88:18). In her essay "On Being Ill," the twentieth-century English novelist Virginia Woolf writes of being sick with influenza, "how we go down into the pit of death and feel the waters of annihilation close above our heads."[13] Woolf is not speaking explicitly of depression here, but she had been struggling with it. It is difficult not to see a connection to her suicide by drowning. The fact that she was sexually abused by her two half-brothers was an obvious factor in Virginia Woolf's mental decline. There are countless other testimonies, of common folk like us and of those who gave public expression to their ordeals by writing about what the poet Adam Zagjewski calls "waves of mute rage."[14]

"When I first became depressed," Jonas says,

I abandoned my contemplative practice for several months. For some reason I felt too raw at the time and feared what wild beasts might be prowling deep down within me. Eventually this calmed down to a certain extent, and I returned to my practice. It was as though I had never stopped practicing. I had abandoned the practice, but the practice had not abandoned me. The practice of contemplation remained the anchor it had always been. Depression remained present, and despite periodic feelings of non-specific rage, low self-esteem, and at times the sense of drowning, the practice of contemplation ultimately revealed something that I don't think I could have realized without the depression. By that I mean that there is something within that is not touched by depression. Depression remains present in my life, but it doesn't dominate my entire being. When I am most silent within, a silence deeper than the lashes of low self-esteem and drowning waves, God's intimate presence allows me not to exert tremendous energy demanding that depression go away. Depression too can be a vehicle of God's presence just like everything else. As odd as it sounds to say it, depression has taught me this. Depression is just as much a vehicle of God's light as joy is.

I can't believe what I am about to say, but clearly depression is the better teacher than joy. I say this simply because I tend to cling to joy. It's more difficult to cling to depression, and pushing it away is not an option for me. If only depression would go away. Nevertheless, depression does not have to go away for us to realize the radiant center embracing all creation. In my case this realization brought with it a certain call to serve others. When I sit on my prayer bench, I sit for all those people who have lost their way in the swelling waters of depression. This has transformed my relationship with depression (difficult as it is). Depression has become my prayer bench and my place of outreach to others just by remaining still. Here I sit in solidarity with all beings, but especially with all those people who are lost in despair. Whether they know it or not, I am here for them.

We have looked at portraits of three people for whom the practice of contemplation does not relieve their depression as it has done for many. Yet the practice of contemplation continues to do its work by gradually removing (decluttering) the illusion of separation from God even when depression stayed on as a more or less permanent, though uninvited, guest. Moreover, Millicent, Brendan, and Jonas lived out of a belief that they came to only gradually: depression became the context for escaping the tyranny of an isolated self, as well as a solid base that tied each to the wider community of those who suffer as they themselves have suffered and continue to suffer. They realized that depression itself can be a vehicle of Light. But the Light does not demand that depression go away if it does not happen to go away. While we always want to seek out various treatment modalities for the healing of depression, when those attempts fail, *we* have not failed, nor are *we* failures. All failure and is grounded in Love. As St. Paul reminds us, the mental distress of depression cannot separate us from the love of God: "What will separate us from the love of Christ? Will anguish, or distress, or persecution, or famine, or nakedness, or peril, or the sword? . . . I am convinced that neither death, nor life, nor angels, nor principalities nor present things, nor future things . . . will be able to separate us from the love of God in Christ Jesus our Lord" (Rom 8:35–39).

All wounds flower. We only need to investigate, by looking straight into the wound. Only interior silence can look deeply into a wound. What silence finds is also silent.

R. S. Thomas draws our attention to this in his poem "Evening":

> Let us stand still, then, in the interval
> of our wounding, till the silence
> turn golden and love is
> a moment eternally overflowing.[15]

The flower of the wound is the flower of awareness that is our grounding essence. The flower of awareness beholds the unity in all the joyous particularities of creation. To perceive with the all-inclusive unity of creation is *to be seen through by love*.

When we sit in silent contemplation, we sit in solidarity with all who suffer affliction. To realize that our pain, though personal, is not private to us is deeply liberating. As we sit on our chair, prayer cushion, or prayer bench or simply lie in bed because at the moment we cannot manage much else, we are free enough, even in the midst of depression that will not budge, to become a gathering place for all who suffer in this life. We become a bridge for all those who have no bridge.

Notes

PREFACE

1. William Faulkner, *Requiem for a Nun* (New York: Vintage Books, 2011), Act 1, Scene 3, 73.

2. Margery Williams, *The Velveteen Rabbit* (New York: George H. Doran, 1922), 5–8.

3. Virginia Woolf, *To the Lighthouse* (New York: Houghton Mifflin Harcourt Publishing Company, 1927), 104–105.

4. *The Cloud of Unknowing*, in *The Cloud of Unknowing and Other Works*, trans. A. C. Spearing (London: Penguin, 2001), ch. 4, 23.

5. Ibid., ch. 6, 27.

6. Ibid., 27–28.

7. Adam Zagajewski, "Transformation," in *Without End: New and Selected Poems*, trans. Clare Cavanagh et al. (New York: Farrar, Straus, and Giroux, 2002), 214.

8. St. Augustine, *Confessions*, 7, 14, trans. Benignus O'Rourke, O.S.A. (London: Darton, Longman, and Todd, 2013), 286.

ONE

1. David Foster Wallace, *This Is Water: Some Thoughts, Delivered on a Significant Occasion About Living a Compassionate Life* (New York: Little, Brown and Company, 2009), 3–4.
2. Ibid., 38.
3. Ibid., 39.
4. Ibid., 44.
5. Ibid., 53.
6. Ibid., 54, 60.
7. Ibid., 82–83.
8. Ibid., 92.
9. Ibid., 89.
10. Ibid., 102.
11. Flannery O'Connor, *A Prayer Journal*, ed. W. A. Sessions (New York: Farrar, Straus, and Giroux, 2013), 3.
12. Howard Thurman, *Temptations of Jesus*, cited in *Howard Thurman: Essential Writings*, ed. Luther E. Smith, Jr. (Maryknoll, NY: Orbis Books, 2006), 45–56.
13. Thomas Merton, "Contemplation in a World of Action," in *Contemplation in a World of Action*, 2nd edition (Notre Dame, IN: University of Notre Dame Press, 2000), 154.
14. Ibid., 154–155.
15. Evagrius Ponticus, "The Praktikos," chs. 43 and 50 in *The Praktikos and Chapters on Prayer*, trans. John Eudes Bamberger (Kalamazoo, MI: Cistercian Publications, 1981), 28, 29–30.
16. Evagrius, "Chapters on Prayer," ch. 70 in *The Praktikos and Chapters on Prayer*, 66; translation altered slightly.
17. Thomas Merton, "Contemplation in a World of Action," 158.
18. Ibid.
19. Ibid., 161.
20. Rowan Williams, https://zenit.org/articles/archbishop-rowan-williams-address-to-the-synod-of-bishops/
21. Ibid., paragraph 5.

22. Ibid., paragraph 8.
23. Ibid., paragraph 8.
24. Merton, "Contemplation in a World of Action," 160.
25. Williams, paragraph 18.
26. *The Cloud of Unknowing*, in *The Cloud of Unknowing and Other Works*, trans. A. C. Spearing (London: Penguin Books, 2001), ch. 3, 22.
27. Elizabeth of the Trinity, Letter 335 in Elizabeth of the Trinity, *Complete Works*, vol. II, trans. Anne England Nash (Washington, DC: ICS Publications, 1995), 360.
28. *Our Thoughts Determine Our Lives: The Life and Teachings of Elder Thaddeus Vitovnica*, compiled by the St. Herman of Alaska Brotherhood, trans. Ana Smiljanic (Platina, CA: St. Herman of Alaska Brotherhood Press, 2012), 63.
29. Ibid.
30. Franz Wright, "Text and Commentary," in *God's Silence* (New York: Alfred A. Knopf, 2008), 64.
31. Elizabeth of the Trinity, "Heaven in Faith," Second Day, in *Collected Works*, vol. I, 96. Here she is quoting from a letter written by Lacordaire to St. Mary Magdalene.
32. St. Augustine, *Confessions* III.vi.7, trans. Henry Chadwick (Oxford: Oxford University Press, 1998), 43 (translation altered slightly).

TWO

1. Plato, *The Republic*, VII, 514a–520a, Loeb Classical Library, ed. and trans. Chris Emlyn-Jones and William Preddy (Cambridge, MA: Harvard University Press, 2013), 118–141.
2. St. Augustine, *Confessions*, 3.4, trans. Chadwick, 43.
3. Meister Eckhart, Sermon 66, in *Meister Eckhart: Sermons and Treatises*, vol. 2, trans. and ed. M. O'C. Walshe (Shaftesbury, Dorset, UK: Element Books, 1979), 139.
4. St. Augustine, *Confessions*, 10, 34, trans. Chadwick, 209.
5. Homily 2, *Homilies on the Song of Songs*, Gregorii Nysseni Opera, ed. H. Langerbeck (Leiden: Brill, 1960), 68, 15–16; translation my own.

6. St. Ambrose, *Hexameron*, in *Corpus Scriptorum Ecclesiasticorum Latinorum*, vol. 32, 1, ed. C. Schenkle (Salzburg, 1897), ch. 10, 75.

7. John Scottus Eriugena, *Homily on the Prologue to the Gospel of John*, 5 in *Celtic Spirituality*, Classics of Western Spirituality, trans. Oliver Davies (New York: Paulist Press, 1999), 414.

8. St. Athanasius the Great, *On the Incarnation*, 57, trans. John Behr (Yonkers, NY: St. Vladimir's Seminary Press, 2011), 167.

9. St. Augustine, *On the Trinity*, X.1, trans. Edmund Hill (Brooklyn, NY: New City Press, 1991), 286.

10. St. Augustine, *Confessions,* I, 1.1, trans. Chadwick, 3.

11. The Pope is quoting almost verbatim Eckhart's Sermon 13b. See *Meister Eckhart: Sermons and Treatises*, vol. 1, 118. The Pope's citation of Eckhart, along with another, occurs in his audience, September 28, 1987, "On the Ecclesial Mission of Adrienne Speyer," cited in "The Eckhart Society Newsletter," see www.eckhart.org/eckhart/eckhart-man.

12. Eckhart, Sermon 13b, *Meister Eckhart: Sermons and Treatises*, vol. 1, 117.

13. Meister Eckhart, Sermon 24, in *Meister Eckhart: Selected Writings*, trans. Oliver Davies, Penguin Classics (London: Penguin Books, 1994), 216.

14. Ibid.

15. Evagrius, *The Praktikos and Chapters on Prayer*, ch. 64, 33–34; translation altered slightly.

16. Eckhart, Sermon 24, *Meister Eckhart: Selected Writings*, 216.

17. Eckhart, Sermon 1, *Meister Eckhart: Sermons and Treatises*, vol. 1, 6–7.

18. John Ruusbroek, "The Little Book of Clarification," in *John Ruusbroeck: The Spiritual Espousal and Other Works*, trans. James Wiseman, The Classics of Western Spirituality (Mahwah, NJ: Paulist Press, 1985), 259.

19. Ibid., "The Sparkling Stone," 159.

20. Ibid., "The Spiritual, Espousels," 75; here Ruusbroec paraphrases St. Augustine, *Confessions* 3.6.

21. St. Catherine of Genoa, *Life and Doctrine of Saint Catherine of Genoa*, ch. 14, translation my own. The Italian reads: *"dico dentro di me: il mio 'me' egli e Dio, ne altro 'me' conosco salvo ch' esso Dio mio."*

22. Teresa of Avila, *The Interior Castle*, trans. Mirabai Starr (New York: River Head Books, 2004), 7.2, 269–270.

23. Ibid., 1.2, 41–42, emphasis added.

24. Ibid., 1.2, 49.

25. St. John of the Cross, "The Living Flame of Love," 1, 12, in *The Collected Works of St. John of the Cross*, trans. Kieran Kavanaugh and Otilio Rodriguez (Washington, DC: Institute of Carmelite Studies, rev. ed., 1991), 645.

26. St. John of the Cross, "The Sayings of Light and Love," in *The Collected Works of St. John of the Cross*, trans. Kieran Kavanaugh and Otilio Rodriguez (Washington, DC: Institute of Carmelite Studies, rev. ed., 1991), 92.

27. St. John of the Cross, "The Living Flame of Love," 2, 10, 661; translation altered slightly.

28. Blessed Elizabeth of the Trinity, Letter 353 in *The Collected Works of Elizabeth of the Trinity*, vol. 2 (Washington, DC: Institute of Carmelite Studies, 1995), 360; emphasis my own.

29. Quoted from *Verses from a Pentecost Novena*; publication details untraceable at this time.

30. Etty Hillesum, cited in *Etty: The Letters and Diaries of Etty Hillesum, 1941–1943, Complete and Unabridged*, ed. Klaas A. D. Smelik and trans. Arnold J. Pomerans (Grand Rapids, MI: William B. Eeerdmans; Novalis, 2002), 60. All citations of Etty Hillesum are taken from this volume.

31. Ibid., 435.

32. Ibid., 60.

33. Ibid., 209.

34. Ibid., 93.

35. Ibid., 126.

36. Ibid., 103. Each of the texts cited here have been helpfully drawn together in the excellent study of Etty Hillesum by Patrick Woodhouse, *Etty Hillesum: A Life Transformed* (London: Bloomsbury, 2009). See also the inspiring selection of her writings, grouped

thematically, by Annemarie S. Kidder, *Etty Hillesum: Essential Writings*, Modern Spiritual Masters Series (Maryknoll, NY: Orbis Books, 2009).

37. Alice Walker, *The Color Purple* (New York: Washington Square Press, 1982), 177.

38. "Emerging," in R. S. Thomas, *Collected Poems 1945–1990* (London: J. M. Dent, 1993), 263.

39. Meister Eckhart, Sermon 13b, *Meister Eckhart: Sermons and Treatises*, 117.

40. Christian Bobin, "The Eighth Day of the Week," cited in *The Eighth Day, Keys to an Open Door, Selected Writings of Christian Bobin*, trans. Pauline Matarasso (London: Darton Longman and Todd, 2015), 24.

41. Ibid., 23, emphasis added.

42. "On Spiritual Knowledge," ch. 29 in *The Philokalia*, vol. 1, trans. and ed. G. E. H. Palmer, Philip Sherrard, and Kallistos Ware (London: Faber and Faber, 1979), 260–261, emphasis added.

43. Ibid.

44. Ibid., 261.

45. Franz Wright, "Scribbled Testament," in *God's Silence* (New York: Alfred A. Knopf), 2008, 138.

46. Christian Bobin, "The Eighth Day of the Week," 24.

47. "On Spiritual Knowledge," ch. 29, 261.

48. I borrow the phrase "stacked up" from Margaret R. Miles in her excellent book, *Beyond the Centaur: Imagining the Intelligent Body* (Eugene, OR: Cascade Books, 2014).

49. Evagrius Ponticus, "Outline Teaching on Asceticism and Stillness in the Solitary Life," in *The Philokalia*, vol. 1, trans. and ed. G. E. H. Palmer, Philip Sherrard, and Kallistos Ware (London: Faber and Faber, 1979), 33.

50. Annie Dillard, *Holy the Firm* (New York: Harper & Row, 1977), 62.

51. John Scottus Eriugena, *Homily on the Prologue to the Gospel of St. John*, trans. Oliver Davies, 414.

THREE

1. Franz Wright, "Scribbled Testament," in *God's Silence* (New York: Alfred A. Knopf, 2006), 138.

2. St. Augustine, *Confessions,* trans. Henry Chadwick, Oxford World Classics (Oxford: Oxford University Press, 1998), III, iv (11), 43.

3. Franz Wright, "Flight," in *Walking to Martha's Vineyard* (New York: Alfred A. Knopf, 2003), 18.

4. Annie Dillard, *Holy the Firm* (New York: Harper and Row, 1977), 24.

5. R. S. Thomas, "Evening," in *Collected Later Poems 1988–2000* (Tarset, Northumberland, UK: Bloodaxe Books, 2004), 223.

6. *The Temple of Our Soul*, trans. Robert Faesen, in *Late Medieval Mysticism of the Low Countries*, ed. Rik Van Nieuwenhove, Robert Faesen, S.J., and Helen Rolfsen, Classics of Western Spirituality (Mahwah, NJ: Paulist Press, 2008), 336.

7. St. Augustine, *Sermons*, Sermon 88.5 in *The Works of St. Augustine*, part 3, book 3, trans. Edmund Hill (Brooklyn, NY: New City Press, 1991), 422; translation altered slightly.

8. *The Evangelical Pearl*, Part III, ch. 5, trans. Helen Rolfson, in *Late Medieval Mysticism of the Low Countries*, ed. Rik Van Nieuwenhove, Robert Faesen, S.J., and Helen Rolfson, Classics of Western Spirituality (Mahwah, NJ: Paulist Press, 2008), 225.

9. St. Diodochos of Photiki, "On Spiritual Knowledge and Discrimination: One Hundred Texts," ch. 25 in *The Philokalia*, vol. 1, trans. Kallistos Ware et al. (London: Faber and Faber, 1979), 259.

10. The term "aesthetic distancing" was coined and developed by the psychologist Adrian van Kaam.

11. St. John Climacus, *The Ladder of Divine Ascent*, Step 27, trans. Colm Luibheid and Norman Russell, Classics of Western Spirituality (Mahwah, NJ: Paulist Press, 1982), 270 (translation slightly altered).

12. St. Hesychios, *On Watchfulness and Holiness*, ch. 2 in *Philokalia*, vol. 1, 162; translation altered slightly.

13. Jan van Ruusbroec, *The Seven Enclosures*, in *The Complete Ruusbroec*, vol. 1, trans. Helen Rolfson, Kees Schepers et al., Corpus

Christianorum Scholars Version (Turnhout, Belgium: Brepols, 2015), 519.

14. Christian Bobin, "A World of Distance," in *The Eighth Day: Keys to an Open Door, Selected Writings of Christian Bobin,* trans. Pauline Matarasso (London: Darton, Longman and Todd, 2015), 62.

15. Franz Wright, "Promise," in *Walking to Martha's Vineyard* (New York: Alfred A. Knopf, 2015), 11.

16. Christian Bobin, *The Lady in White*, trans. Alison Anderson (Lincoln: University of Nebraska Press, 2014), 12.

17. Christian Bobin, "A World of Difference," in *The Eighth Day*, 62.

18. David Whyte, "Midsummer Prayer," in *River Flow: New and Selected Poems,* rev. ed. (Langley, WA: Many Rivers Press, 2012), 49.

19. Evagrius Ponticus, *Praktikos*, ch. 43 in *The Praktikos and Chapters on Prayer*, trans. John Eudes (Kalamazoo, MI: Cistercian Publications, 1981), 28.

20. Franz Wright, "The New Jerusalem," in *Walking to Martha's Vineyard* (New York: Alfred A. Knopf, 2015), 63.

21. Evagrius, *Praktikos,* ch. 48, in *The Praktikos and Chapters on Prayer*, 28, translation altered slightly.

22. Ibid., translation altered slightly.

23. St. Augustine, Sermon 160, 13, trans. Edmund Hill, *Sermons*, in *The Works of St. Augustine*, III/1 (New Rochelle, NY: New City Press), 231.

24. Bobin, "The Eighth Day of the Week," in *The Eighth Day*, 24.

25. St. Teresa of Avila, *The Interior Castle*, I, 2, trans. Mirabai Starr (New York: Riverhead Books, 2003), 42.

26. Ibid.

27. *The Cloud of Unknowing*, ch. 7, in *The Cloud of Unknowing and Other Works*, trans. A. C. Spearing (London: Penguin Books, 2001), 29.

28. Evagrius, "Chapters on Prayer," ch. 43, in *The Praktikos and Chapters on Prayer*, 61–62; translation altered slightly.

29. Ruusbroec, *The Seven Enclosures*, 519.

FOUR

1. St. John of the Cross, *The Spiritual Canticle*, Red A., str. 38. I cite a translation from an older version of *The Liturgy of the Hours*, Office of Readings for the Feast of St. John of the Cross, December 14.

2. Eckhart, Sermon 13b, *Sermons and Treatises*, vol. 1, 117.

3. Franz Wright, "The Walk," in *The Silence of God* (New York: Alfred A. Knopf, 2006), 76.

4. St. Bonaventure, "*de incurvatus in se,*" in *Opera Omnia Doctoris Seraphici S. Bonaventurae* (Quarrachi, Italy: Collegium S. Bonaventurae, vol. 2, 635 *et passim*).

5. Kevin Hart, "Prayer," in *Morning Knowledge* (Notre Dame, IN: University of Notre Dame Press, 2011), 37.

6. Martin Laird, O.S.A., "Continually Breathe Jesus Christ: Stillness and Watchfulness in the *Philokalia*," *Communio* 34 (2007): 243–263.

7. For a glimpse of how the medical community is interested in the effects of spirituality on health see, *inter al.*, Harold Koenig, *Medicine, Religion and Health: Where Science and Spirituality Meet* (West Conshohocken, PA: Templeton Foundation Press, 2008).

8. *The Art of Prayer: An Orthodox Anthology*, compiled by Igumen Chariton of Valamo, trans. E. Kadloubovski and E. M. Palmer, ed. Timothy Ware (London: Faber and Faber, 1966), 90.

9. St. Teresa of Avila, *The Interior Castle*, IV, 3, trans. Mirabai Starr (New York: Riverhead Books, 2003), 107; translation altered slightly.

10. *The Cloud of Unknowing*, in *The Cloud of Unknowing and Other Works*, trans. A. C. Spearing (London: Penguin Books, 2001), ch. 7, 29.

11. Ibid.

12. Ibid.

13. Ibid.

14. Ibid., ch. 32, 55.

15. Eckhart, Sermon 29, *Sermons and Treatises*, vol. 1, trans. and ed. M. O'C. Walshe (Shaftesbury, Dorset, UK: Element Books, 1987), 216.

16. Evagrius, *Chapters on Prayer*, ch. 72, trans. John Eudes Bamberger (Kalamazoo, MI: Cistercian Publications, 1981), 67; translation adapted to first-person plural. In the context of his day, Evagrius was combating a resurgence of the anthropomorphite heresy among certain monks. This heresy holds that God looks like a human being, the man with a white beard, so to speak.

17. Evagrius, *Chapters on Prayer*, ch. 70, 66; translation altered slightly.

18. St. Gregory of Nyssa, *Life of Moses*, II, 165, trans. Abraham Mahlerbee (Mahwah, NJ: Paulist Press, 1978), 96; slight synthetic paraphrasing.

19. Angelus Silesius, "Ohne warum," in *Cherubinischer Wandersmann* (Bremen: Carl Schünemann Verlag, no publication date given), 37 (translation my own).

20. See St. Augustine, *On the Trinity*, X.1, trans. Edmund Hill (Brooklyn, NY: New City Press), 287.

21. St. Gregory of Nyssa, *Life of Moses*, II, 163, 95.

22. Christian Bobin, "Mozart and the Rain," in *The Eighth Day,* 71.

23. Christian Bobin, "A World of Distance," in *The Eighth Day,* 62.

24. My thanks to Brian D. Robinette for leading me to this insight by Karl Rahner, *Foundations of Christian Faith: An Introduction to the Idea of Christianity*, trans. William Dych (New York: Crossroad), 62; Brian D. Robinette, "Undergoing Something from Nothing: Creation as Contemplative Insight," in *The Practice of the Presence of God: Theology as a Way of Life,* ed. Martin Laird and Sheelah Treflé Hidden (London: Routledge, 2017), 21–23.

25. St. John of the Cross, *The Living Flame of Love*, 1, 12, in *The Collected Works of St. John of the Cross*, trans. Kieran Kavanaugh and Otilio Rodriguez (Washington, DC: Institute of Carmelite Studies, 1991, rev. ed.), 645.

FIVE

1. Symeon the New Theologian, *The Practical and Theological Chapters*, 2.16, in *The Practical and Theological Chapters and the Three Theological Discourses*, trans. Paul McGuckin (Kalamazoo, MI: Cistercian Publications, 1982), 67.

2. Ibid.; translation altered slightly.

3. St. Symeon the New Theologian, *The Practical and Theological Chapters*, 2.17, 67; translation altered slightly.

4. St. Athanasius, *On the Incarnation*, 54.3, trans. John Behr (Yonkers, NY: St. Vladimir's Seminary Press, 2011), 167; translation altered slightly.

5. See St. Teresa of Avila, *The Interior Castle*, 7.2, trans. Mirabai Starr (New York: Riverhead Books), 270.

6. Howard Thurman, cited in Luther E. Smith, Jr., *Howard Thurman: The Mystic as Prophet* (Richmond, IN: Friends United Press, 3rd ed., 2007), 174–175.

7. St. John of the Cross, *The Spiritual Canticle*, Red A, strophe 38.

8. Eckhart, Sermon 24, *Meister Eckhart: Selected Writings*, trans. Oliver Davies (London: Penguin), 216.

9. Howard Thurman, "Temptations of Jesus," cited in *Howard Thurman: Essential Writings*, ed. Luther E. Smith, Jr. (Maryknoll, NY: Orbis Books, 2006), 46.

10. Ibid.

11. Howard Thurman, *Deep River*, cited in *Howard Thurman: Essential Writings*, ed. Luther E. Smith, Jr. (Maryknoll, NY: Orbis Books, 2006), 40. In light of today's sensitivities to sexist language, Thurman's use of the male pronoun in an inclusive sense can be jarring to some. In his day there was nothing remarkable about this. However, The Thurman Estates stipulates that Thurman be quoted exactly how he wrote it. Hence, we honor the request of his Estate.

12. Eckhart, Sermon 24, *Meister Eckhart: Selected Writings*, 216.

13. Eckhart, Sermon 24, *Meister Eckhart: Selected Writings*, 217.

14. John Chapman, *Spiritual Letters* (London: Sheed and Ward, 1935), 176.

15. St. John of the Cross, "The Sayings of Light and Love," 138, in *The Collected Works of St. John of the Cross* (Washington, DC: Institute of Carmelite Studies, rev. ed., 1991), 95; translation altered slightly.

16. St. John of the Cross, "The Ascent of Mount Carmel," Bk. 1, ch. 13, in *The Collected Works*, 150.

17. *Our Thoughts Determine Our Lives: The Life and Teaching of Elder Thaddeus of Vitovnica,* trans. Ana Smiljinac (Platina, CA: Saint Herman of Alaska Brotherhood, 2017), 133.

18. *The Cloud of Unknowing,* in *The Cloud of Unknowing and Other Works,* trans. A. C. Spearing (London: Penguin Classics, 2001), ch. 7, 29.

19. *The Cloud of Unknowing,* ch. 32, 55.

20. St. Augustine, *Confessions*, XIII, ix, 10, trans. Henry Chadwick (Oxford: Oxford University Press, 1991), 278.

21. Madeleine Delbrêl, *Alcide: Guide simple pour simples chrétiens* (Paris: Éditions du Seuil, 1968), 23 (translation my own).

22. Angelus Selisius, *Cherubinischer Wandersmann*, I, 289, (Carl Schünemann Verlag, no publication year given), 37 (translation my own).

23. St. Hesychios the Priest, "On Watchfulness and Holiness," 139, in *The Philokalia*, vol. 1, trans. and ed. Kallistos Ware et al. (London: Faber and Faber, 1979), 185.

24. St. John of the Cross, "Sayings of Light and Love," 56, in *Collected Works*, 89.

25. Howard Thurman, "Temptations of Jesus," in *Howard Thurman: Essential Writings*, 46.

26. St. Gregory of Nyssa, *Homelies on the Song of Songs*, Homily 11, trans. Casimir McCambley (Brookline, MA: Hellenic College Press, 1987), 203.

27. Evagrius, "Chapters on Prayer," in *The Praktikos and Chapters on Prayer*, 125, 76.

28. John Chapman, *Spiritual Letters* (London: Sheed and Ward, 1935), 176–177.

29. Hadewijch of Brabant, Letter 6, 86, in *Hadewijch: The Complete Works*, trans. Mother Columba Hart, O.S.B. (Mahwah, NJ: Paulist Press, 1980), 58.

SIX

1. For a recent presentation of this and much more, see the excellent book by Daniel Goleman and Richard J. Davidson, *Altered Traits: Science*

Reveals How Meditation Changes Your Mind, Brain, and Body (New York: Penguin Random House, 2017).

2. *The Cloud of Unknowing*, ch. 54 in *The Cloud of Unknowing and Other Works*, trans. A. C. Spearing (London: Penguin Books, 2001), 78.

3. "A Letter of Private Direction," V, in *The Pursuit of Wisdom and Other Works by the Author of The Cloud of Unknowing*, trans. and ed. James Walsh, S. J. (New York: Paulist Press, 1988), 230.

4. Franz Wright, "Pediatric Suicide," in *Wheeling Motel* (New York: Alfred A. Knopf, 2009; 2017), 22.

5. Wendell Miles, in Margaret R. Miles, *The Wendell Cocktail: Depression, Addiction, and Beauty* (Eugene, OR: Cascade Books, 2012), 30.

6. Franz Wright, "The Visiting," in *God's Silence* (New York: Alfred A. Knopf, 2008), 119.

7. "I Wake and Feel," in *Gerard Manley Hopkins: The Major Works*, ed. Catherine Phillips (Oxford: Oxford University Press, 2009), 166. Hopkins struggled with depression for long periods of his life. Poetry's politesse permits him a creative outlet that does not free him from depression but gives us insight into the ordeal that is depression.

8. J. D. Salinger, *Franny and Zooey* (Boston: Little, Brown and Company, 1961), 15–16.

9. William Styron, *Darkness Visible: A Memoir of Madness* (New York: Vintage Books, 1992), 7.

10. Rainer Maria Rilke, Letter dated July 16, 1903, in *A Year with Rilke,* trans. and ed. Joanna Macy and Anita Barrows (New York: HarperCollins, 2009), 18; compare the translation by M. D. Herter Norton, *Letters to a Young Poet* (New York: W.W. Norton and Company, rev. ed. 1954), 35.

11. "No Worst," in *Gerard Manley Hopkins: The Major Works*, ed. Catherine Phillips (Oxford: Oxford University Press, 2009), 167. See the sensitive study by Hilary E. Pearson, "The 'Terrible Sonnets' of Gerard Manley Hopkins and the Spirituality of Depression," *The Way* 46/1 (January 2007), 23–27.

12. St. Augustine, *Exposition of Psalm 60*, in *Expositions of the Psalms*, Part III, vol. 17, trans. Dame Maria Boulding, O.S.B. (Hyde Park, NY: New City Press, 2001), 194 (translation altered slightly).

13. Virginia Woolf, "On Being Ill," in *The Crowded Dance of Modern Life*, ed. Rachel Bowlby (London: Penguin Books, 1993), 43.

14. Adam Zagajewski, "Three Angels," in *New and Selected Poems* (New York: Farrar, Strauss and Giroux, 2002), 266.

15. R. S. Thomas, "Evening," in *Collected Later Poems 1988–2000* (Tarset, Northumberland, UK: Blood Axe Books, 2004), 223.